Three Cheers *for* Pooh

'Oh, Bear!' said
Christopher Robin.
'How I do love you!'
'So do I,' said Pooh.

Three Cheers for Pooh

A Celebration of the Best Bear in All the World

by Brian Sibley

EGMONT

For my good friend
ANTONY MIALL
who I first met when he was seated at a piano
playing and singing The Hums of Pooh,
and in grateful memory of
Mrs Bertoletti, Miss Baker and Mr Bull

Three Cheers for Pooh
First published in October 2001 under the Methuen imprint by Egmont Children's Books Limited.
This edition first published 2006 by Egmont UK Limited
239 Kensington High Street, London W8 6SA

Hand lettering by Carol Kemp.

A CIP catalogue record for this title is available from the British Library.

ISBN 978 1 4052 2911 1
ISBN 1 4052 2911 X

1 3 5 7 9 10 8 6 4 2

Printed and bound in Singapore

Contents

That Sort of Bear!

3 Cheers for Pooh! (For who?)
For Pooh — (Why what did he do?)
I thought you knew . . .

Now and again when Pooh is on his way to and from some-where else, he stops at that warm and sunny Thoughtful Spot where he sometimes meets Piglet (being, as it is, half-way between Pooh's house and Piglet's house) and he has a Think.

The trouble is, 'when you are a Bear of Very Little Brain, and you Think of Things, you find sometimes that a Thing which seemed very Thingish inside you is quite different when it gets out into the open and has other people looking at it'.

For example, didn't Christopher Robin once say that Pooh was the Best Bear in All the World? And wasn't it Rabbit who once had an Idea for an Adventure that would be Impossible Without Pooh? And mightn't it have been Owl who called him an Astute and Helpful Bear — or was it *Stout* and Helpful? Well, anyway, Somebody did.

For this is 'Winnie-the-Pooh, F.O.P. (Friend of Piglet's), R.C. (Rabbit's Companion), P.D. (Pole Discoverer), E.C. and T.F. (Eeyore's Comforter and Tail-finder)'.

Pooh: who invented the game of Poohsticks and made up all kinds of Good Hums, such as are Hummed Hopefully to Others; who devised those vessels, *The Floating Bear* (which was Sometimes a Boat and sometimes more of an Accident) and *The Brain of Pooh* (*Captain*, C. Robin; *1st Mate*, P. Bear).

Pooh: who co-incidentally discovered the North Pole and, at the same time, saved Roo from drowning (though Roo says he was *swimming*); who rescued Piglet (who is a Very Small Animal) when he was Entirely Surrounded by Water (and *couldn't* swim) and who found Small (who is an even Smaller Animal) when he was Lost.

Pooh: who practised a deception on the wrong sort of bees; who tracked a couple of Woozles – and one, as it might be, Wizzle – in the snow; who thought up a Cunning Trap for Heffalumps and accidentally caught himself.

It is true that Pooh can never resist a little Smackerel of Something around about eleven o'clock; and, yes, Eeyore *did* once call him a Bear with a Pleasing Manner but a Positively Startling Lack of Brain. But still we say:

3 Cheers for the wonderful Winnie-the-Pooh!
(*Just tell me, somebody* – WHAT DID HE DO?)

Which is precisely why we have written this book.

The Handsome Cub

'Pooh, promise you won't forget about me, ever.
Not even when I'm a hundred.'
Pooh thought for a little. 'How old shall I be then?'
'Ninety-nine.' Pooh nodded.

Go into any toyshop and survey the serried ranks of teddy bears. At first glance they all look much the same. But look again and you will see that they all have their own distinguishing characteristics: that one in the front has a rather gruff expression and that one on the right is clearly a lovable bear, while the one behind him appears positively stupid! But *that* bear – the one over there, on the left, second from the end – has a very special look about him: the sort of Bear who might not necessarily have been Born Great, but who will either Achieve Greatness or have Greatness Thrust Upon Him!

It was just such a bear, a handsome fellow in golden mohair, that, in August 1921, was purchased from the toy department of Harrods in London by Mrs Daphne Milne as a first birthday present for her son, named Christopher Robin, but known to the family as 'Billy Moon'.

Winnie-the-Pooh, 'V. I. B.' (Very Important Bear): Pooh sits for society photographer, Marcus Adams, in 1928.

A blue plaque at 11 (now number 13) Mallord Street, Chelsea, marks the home of A. A. Milne, Christopher Robin and Pooh.

Mrs Milne carried the Bear home to 11 Mallord Street, Chelsea, and doubtless showed her purchase, with some pride, to her husband, Alan, who, as A. A. Milne, was already well-established as a successful playwright and humorist. Mr Milne may not have immediately recognised the furry newcomer's literary potential (and it was to be some years before he became known as Winnie-the-Pooh), but one-year-old Billy loved his Bear from the very first. 'Every child has his favourite toy,' he was to write many years after, 'and every only-child has a special need of one. Pooh was mine.'

So that's how Pooh came into the story, but it is not where the story truly begins. That starts on 18 January 1882, with the birth of Alan Alexander Milne, third son (after Barry and Ken) of John Vine Milne and his wife, Sarah. As A. A. Milne later put it: '"Once upon a time there was a man who had three sons" – this was how we began, this was how the fairy stories began.'

Alan's father, the son of a Scottish Congregational missionary, had been born in Jamaica. Largely self-educated, J. V. Milne ran a small private school in Kilburn, London, where Alan received his earliest education. H. G. Wells who was, for a time, one of the masters, confidently (but wrongly) predicted that young Alan would make a career in mathematics.

'What's twice eleven?' I said to Pooh,
('Twice what?' said Pooh to Me.)

J. V. Milne wrote of his son and pupil: 'Thinks mathematics grand. He leaves his books

John Vine Milne and his three sons: Barry on the left, Ken on the right and, sitting in front, Alan Alexander. 'I had blue eyes and flaxen hair,' wrote A. A. Milne of his young self, 'these were the Little Lord Fauntleroy days and on occasions I wore a velvet suit and lace collar.'

about; loses his pen; can't imagine what he did with this, and where he put that, but is convinced that it is somewhere . . . Can speak 556 words per minute, and writes more in three minutes than his instructor can read in thirty.'

Though fifteen months younger than Ken, Alan was devoted to his older brother and they remained close companions until Ken's death in 1929. The friendship between Pooh and Piglet owes much to the special relationship between Alan and Ken: 'they began to talk in a friendly way about this and that, and Piglet said, "If you see what I mean, Pooh," and Pooh said, "It's just what I think myself, Piglet," and Piglet said, "But, on the other hand, Pooh, we must remember," and Pooh said, "Quite true, Piglet, although I had forgotten it for the moment."'

Friends and brothers: Alan and Ken Milne as drawn by E. H. Shepard for A. A. Milne's childhood memoir, *When I Was Very Young* (1930).

At the age of eleven, Milne won a scholarship to Westminster School where Ken was already a student. Using the initials 'A. K. M.', the two brothers began writing light verse together for the school magazine, *The Elizabethan*. The versifier of *When We Were Very Young* and *Now We Are Six* was already finding his measure:

> Shall I write you a parody, smart and satirical,
> After the manner of *Punch* and the rest –
> Or something in dialect pretty and lyrical,
> Safe to remind you of Burns at his best?

> Perhaps you would fancy an 'Ode to an Eider-duck'
> Telling his praises with never a pause:
> How he was born a duck, lived – yes, and died a duck,
> Hampered by Nature's inscrutable laws.

One day at school, young Alan chanced upon a copy of *Granta*, the Cambridge undergraduate magazine, and, when a friend suggested that he ought to go to Cambridge and edit it, he calmly replied that he *would*. So he *did*!

It was 1900 when Alan went up to Trinity College, Cambridge and, two years later, he was duly editing *Granta*, with rather more success than he achieved in his studies. His father had hoped Alan would get a First Class degree, Alan himself would have settled for a Second, but, alas:

The work we did was rarely reckoned
Worthy a Tutor's kindly word,
For when I said we got a Second
I really meant we got a Third . . .

Still, he had had fun, proved to himself that he could write and, after all, as Eeyore would remark: 'Education! What *is* learning?'

Leaving Cambridge in 1903, and ignoring his father's advice to go into either the Civil Service or teaching, Alan set off for London in pursuit of his ambition to be a writer. He took rooms in Bouverie Street, so as to be near the offices of the humorous magazine, *Punch*, and began bombarding newspapers and journals with stories, essays and verses. Eventually he succeeded in selling one to *Vanity Fair* and duly received a cheque for 15/- (75 pence).

And eventually, *Punch* accepted no less than three contributions and, by the end of his first year as a freelance journalist, he had earned the princely sum of £20. Two years later, in 1906, *Punch* got a new editor, Owen Seaman, who offered the twenty-four-year-old Alan Milne the job of Assistant Editor, on a salary of £250 a year. He could now seriously think of himself as a real writer.

Week by week, the young Mr Milne contributed light-hearted pieces to *Punch*, seemingly thrown off with effortless charm: 'Sometimes when the printer is waiting for an article which really should have been sent to him the day before, I sit at my desk and wonder if there is anything I can possibly find to say . . .'

But, somehow, he always did: 'Let us talk about – well, anything

14

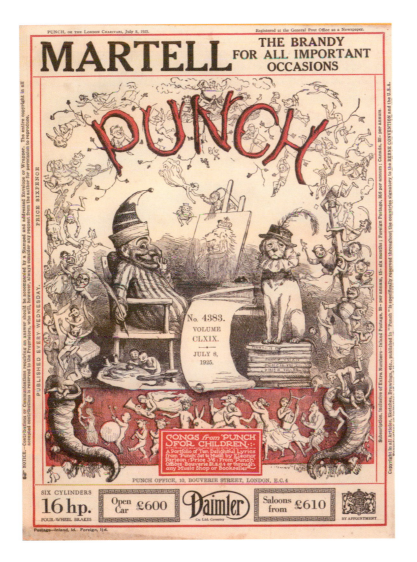

Richard Doyle's famous cover design for *Punch*, the magazine that launched Milne's career as a writer. It was in the pages of *Punch*, that Winnie-the-Pooh (then known as 'Teddy Bear') would eventually make his debut.

you will. Goldfish, for instance . . .' Or lots of other subjects; many of them involving the kind of muddly confusions which later got entangled in the conversations of Pooh:

'The other day I met a man who didn't know where Tripoli was. Tripoli happened to come into the conversation, and he was evidently at a loss. "Let's see," he said. "Tripoli is just down by the – er –

you know. What's the name of that place?" "That's right," I answered, "just opposite Thingumabob. I could show you in a minute on the map. It's near – what do they call it?" At this moment the train stopped, and I got out and went straight home to look at an atlas . . .'

Collections of Milne's essays and articles appeared in a series of best-selling volumes with such jolly titles as *The Sunny Side*, *Not That It Matters* and *If I May*. Milne had also begun experimenting with play-writing, beginning with *Make-Believe*, a one-act entertainment for children.

In 1913, Alan Milne met and married Dorothy de Selincourt (known as Daphne for short, or Daff for shorter) who was god-daughter of the editor of *Punch*. 'She laughed at my jokes,' said Milne, and it was for Daphne, that he wrote what might be called his first children's book, except that *he* said it was really intended 'for those, young or old, who like the things which I like.'

Once On A Time, published in 1917, was a story about how life in Fairyland was 'not as straightforward as the romancers pretend'. It was full of fairy-tale folk who were really just like the rest of us, except that they lived in a world cluttered up with magic. Mr Milne was developing a quirky way of looking at things.

The First World War brought a short interruption to Milne's writing career: he joined the Royal Warwickshire Regiment as a signals officer and later served on the Somme, until invalided out with trench-fever. It was a period of his life that he loathed and which, rather remarkably, he managed to endure without losing his sense of humour:

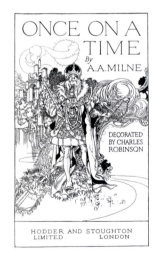

Once On A Time was first published in 1917. This 1925 edition was illustrated by Charles Robinson.

Daphne and Alan Milne
in 1925.

'When the war is over and we've finished up the show,
I'm going to plant a lemon pip and listen to it grow . . .'

Wurzel-Flummery, a two-act play which Milne had written just before being posted to France, was produced in London in 1917, on the same bill as plays by Milne's idol, J. M. Barrie. It told the improbable story of Robert Crawshaw, a pompous Member of Parliament, bequeathed the fabulous sum of £50,000, on the 'trifling condition' that he adopt the ridiculous name 'Wurzel-Flummery'! Less than ten years later the same author would be inventing 'Woozles' and 'Heffalumps'!

'. . . every Heffalump that he counted was making straight for a pot of Pooh's honey, *and eating it all.*'

More plays followed and, by the early 'twenties, Milne was already well-known as the author of a string of theatrical successes such as *Mr Pim Passes By* and *The Truth About Blaydes*. He had also written *Toad of Toad Hall*, a stage version of one of his favourite books, *The Wind in the Willows* by Kenneth Grahame. By the time the play was eventually staged, in 1929, Mr Milne was even more famous as a children's author than Mr Grahame.

At eight o'clock on the morning of 21 August 1920, Mrs Milne gave birth to a baby. It was an event without which Mr Milne might never have achieved that fame.

'We had intended to call it Rosemary,' Milne was to recall, 'but decided later that Billy would be more suitable. However, as you can't be christened William – at least we didn't see why anybody should – we had to think of two other names . . . One of us thought of Robin, the other of Christopher; names wasted on him who called himself "Billy Moon" as soon as he could talk and has been "Moon" to his family and friends ever since.' No wonder the grown-up Christopher later complained of having suffered from 'an embarrassment of names'.

In the Milne family, names were always a complicated business. On A. A. Milne's own birth, his father initially registered him as 'Alan Sydney', only to change his names, a few days later, to 'Alan Alexander'. And, like Billy, Alan was never known to his family and friends by his given names, but always as 'Blue', his favourite colour and, incidentally, that of his eyes.

As for the famous names by which his son would eventually be known all over the world, they had been chosen, according to A. A. Milne, in order to encourage the boy to 'make his name in the sporting world'. After all, might not 'C. R. Milne', rather like W. G. Grace and C. B. Fry, one day play cricket for England?

It was on Billy's first birthday in 1921, that the bear arrived and, as it happened, he *also* had several names, and would later acquire even

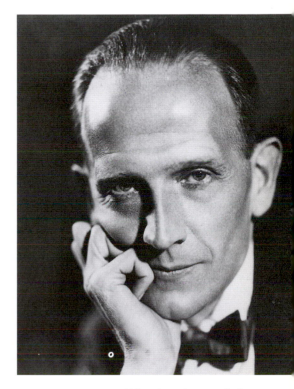

Although rarely at ease before the camera, A. A. Milne looks relaxed and confident in this photograph taken at the height of his fame, by Howard Coster.

more! To begin with he was sometimes known as 'Big Bear' or as 'Mr Edward' or, quite simply, by the name with which he was to make his literary debut – 'Teddy Bear'.

Over the years, Christopher Robin's nursery companion has inspired a great many cuddly toys. Here, a clutch of contemporary Pooh Bears flank a veteran Winnie-the-Pooh (sporting a blue jacket), who was modelled on E. H. Shepard's illustrations and specially made for 'Pooh's Christmas at Heals', an event held at the London store in 1969.

Our Teddy Bear is Short and Fat

Now tubbiness is just the thing
Which gets a fellow wondering;
And Teddy worried lots about
The fact that he was rather stout.

Teddy was just one year younger than the boy *we* know as Christopher Robin, (but who called *himself* 'Billy Moon'), and he had quickly established himself as part of the family. 'The bear took his place in the nursery,' recalled the adult Christopher, 'and gradually he began to come to life . . .'

That life was a private affair, known only to the child and his parents, until Christopher's father started writing verses, hums and songs for children. Although A. A. Milne had been writing 'light verse', as it was called, for years ('It isn't Brain . . . but it comes to me sometimes'), it was always aimed at grown-up readers. Then, one day, he wrote a verse that wasn't exactly meant *for* a child, but which was certainly *about* a child.

'Time for a little something':
Winnie-the-Pooh and
Christopher Robin,
photographed by
Marcus Adams in 1928.

Passing the open door to his son's nursery, Milne looked in and saw the young boy, kneeling beside his bed. Under the supervision of his Nanny, Olive Rand, Christopher was saying his prayers. Milne retired to his study and wrote a poem about it:

> Little Boy kneels at the foot of the bed,
> Droops on the little hands little gold head.
> Hush! Hush! Whisper who dares!
> Christopher Robin is saying his prayers.

Mother and son (with bear): Marcus Adams asked Daphne Milne to join Christopher and Pooh for this photograph.

Milne called it 'Vespers' and gave it to his wife, telling her that if she could sell it, she could keep the publication fee. So Daphne Milne sent the verse to the New York periodical, *Vanity Fair*, who paid her $50 and published the poem in the January 1923 issue.

The name 'Christopher Robin' had found its way into print and that might easily have been the end of it, but for an invitation to write some children's verses for *The Merry-Go-Round*, a new magazine that was to be edited by Rose Fyleman, the author of, among other things, a poem which began: 'There are fairies at the bottom of my garden . . .'

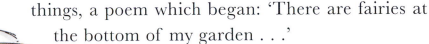

Milne was not enthusiastic: 'I said that I didn't and couldn't, it wasn't in my line.' However, as he later explained, 'as soon as I'd posted my letter, I did what I always do after refusing to write anything: wondered how I would have written it if I hadn't refused.' He might, for example, have written:

There once was a Dormouse who lived in a bed
Of delphiniums (blue) and geraniums (red),
And all the day long he'd a wonderful view
Of geraniums (red) and delphiniums (blue).

The poem was 'The Dormouse and the Doctor' and Miss
Fyleman eagerly accepted it for publication.

It was summer, and it was raining. 'It rained and
it rained and it rained. Piglet told himself that
never in all his life, and *he* was goodness knows *how*
old – three, was it, or four? – never had he seen
so much rain. Days and days and days.'

Alan and Daphne Milne (accompanied by
Billy and his Teddy Bear) were at a house
party in Wales, at Llanfrothen, near Portmadoc.
Milne was getting very bored with being cooped
up indoors with nothing in particular to do. Then, one
morning, he received a package from Rose Fyleman containing the
proofs of the 'Dormouse' poem and a note suggesting that he ought to
write a whole book of such verses.

'The Doctor stood frowning
and shaking his head . . .'
Illustration by E. H. Shepard
for Milne's verse about 'The
Dormouse and the Doctor'.

Since it was still pouring with rain, Milne retired to a summer-
house in the garden, intending to go over the proofs. When he'd
finished, he started work on another poem. And then another.

'There I was,' he wrote later, 'with an exercise book and a
pencil, and a fixed determination not to leave the heavenly solitude of
that summer-house until it stopped raining . . . and there on the other
side of the lawn was a child with whom I had lived for three years . . .

24

and here within me were unforgettable memories of my own childhood . . . what was I writing? A child's book of verses obviously. Not a whole book, of course; but to write a few would be fun – until I tired of it. Besides, my pencil had an India-rubber at the back; just the thing for poetry . . .'

Of course, it wasn't that easy, as Pooh would say: 'Because Poetry and Hums aren't things which you get, they're things which get *you*. And all you can do is to go where they can find you.'

Eleven wet days later, there were eleven sets of verses. Back in London, Milne found himself writing more and more poems, until, by the end of the year, there were enough to make a book.

Some of the poems were specifically about Billy – or, as he would now be better known, Christopher Robin: 'You will have noticed,' Milne wrote, 'that the words "Christopher Robin" come trippingly off the tongue. I noticed that too. You simply can't sit down to write verses for children, in a house with a child called (however officially only) Christopher Robin, without noticing it.'

Other verses, whilst they seemed to be about Christopher Robin, were actually rather more autobiographical: 'As a child I kept a mouse; probably it escaped – they generally do. Christopher Robin has kept almost everything except a mouse. As a child I played lines-and-squares in a casual sort of way. Christopher Robin never did until he read what I had written about it, and not very enthusiastically then.'

Portrait of Christopher Robin (opposite) used as a frontispiece to a 1925 American edition of *When We Were Very Young.*

There was also, *at last*, a poem about Billy's bear:

> A bear, however hard he tries,
> Grows tubby without exercise.
> Our Teddy Bear is short and fat,
> Which is not to be wondered at;
> He gets what exercise he can
> By falling off the ottoman,
> But generally seems to lack
> The energy to clamber back.

The ottoman, which stood under the nursery window in 11 Mallord Street, Chelsea, was home to Christopher's toys:

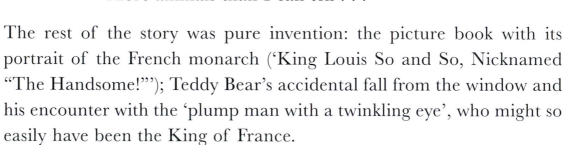

> Now Teddy, as was only right,
> Slept in the ottoman at night,
> And with him crowded in as well
> More animals than I can tell . . .

The rest of the story was pure invention: the picture book with its portrait of the French monarch ('King Louis So and So, Nicknamed "The Handsome!"'); Teddy Bear's accidental fall from the window and his encounter with the 'plump man with a twinkling eye', who might so easily have been the King of France.

Milne sent 'Teddy Bear' and all the other poems to his publishers, Methuen, who had actually been hoping for a long-awaited sequel to a highly successful detective story, which Milne had written a few years earlier.

Children's poetry was rarely a big seller, but Methuen's Managing Director, E. V. Lucas, happened to be a former Deputy Editor of *Punch* and he hit on a Good Idea: if *Punch* previewed the verses, then it would help eventual sales of the book. The magazine agreed and it was decided that the verses should be illustrated by one of *Punch's* regular artists, E. H. Shepard.

Although Milne knew Shepard's work from his own days on *Punch*, he held a poor view of the artist and used to ask the magazine's art editor: 'What on earth do you see in this man? He's perfectly hopeless.' Aware, perhaps, of Milne's negative views, Shepard approached the task of illustrating *When We Were Very Young* with some trepidation: 'It is,' he wrote years later, 'anxious work making pictures of an author's written words, and when I took my first sketches to show Alan Milne, I had some nervous moments while he studied them. It was clear he was pleased and, when he had seen them all, he said, "They are fine, go right ahead." Then added, "There will be about fifty altogether, you know."'

E. H. Shepard was born in London, in 1879 (three years before Milne), and went to St Paul's School. A lively lad with a fondness for practical jokes,

Among the first poems which the artist, E. H. Shepard received was 'Teddy Bear': 'I realised,' said Shepard 'what a grand time was ahead of me.'

Self-portrait of the artist as a young man: E. H. Shepard in about 1900.

young Ernest Howard was dubbed – in the slang of his day – a 'giddy kipper' and, thereafter, was known to family and friends as 'Kipper' or, simply, 'Kip'.

Shepard studied at Heatherley's School of Fine Art and the Royal Academy Schools. After distinguished service in the First World War (rising to the rank of Major and being awarded the Military Cross), he became a regular contributor to *Punch*.

Whatever reservations Milne had once had about Shepard, the artist perfectly caught the spirit of his verses in drawings that are full of fun and nonsense and superb observation of child behaviour.

After toying with various possible titles – *A Nursery Window Box*, *Swings and Roundabouts* and *Buttercups and Daisies* – Milne finally decided to call the collection *When We Were Very Young*, and the verses began making their appearance in *Punch* during January 1924 with 'Teddy Bear' taking his bow the following month. Surrounded with wonderful Shepard drawings, the poems made a big impact and, when the book was published the following November, there was little doubt that it was going to be a success. 'It is,' wrote one critic, 'a book that all children will adore. It is a book that mothers and nurses will laugh and cry over. It is a – classic!'

Among Shepard's illustrations was a picture of the author (pipe in mouth) heading off with Christopher Robin 'down to the shouting sea' in the poem 'Sand-between-the-toes'. Although Teddy Bear was only featured in one of the *When We Were Very Young* poems, Shepard

Ernest Shepard was a master at observing and capturing child behaviour and once said that children were his favourite subject. His son, Graham, was the inspiration and model for many of the drawings in *When We Were Very Young* that we now think of as being pictures of 'Christopher Robin' Milne.

28

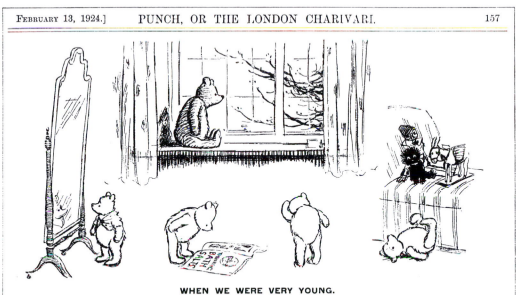

WHEN WE WERE VERY YOUNG.

IX.—TEDDY BEAR.

A BEAR, however hard he tries,
Grows tubby without exercise.
Our Teddy Bear is short and fat,
Which is not to be wondered at;
He gets what exercise he can
By falling off the ottoman,
But generally seems to lack
The energy to clamber back.

Now tubbiness is just the thing
Which gets a fellow wondering;
And Teddy worried lots about
The fact that he was rather stout.
He thought: "If only I were thin!
But how does anyone begin?"
He thought: "It really isn't fair
To grudge me exercise and air."

For many weeks he pressed in vain
His nose against the window-pane,
And envied those who walked
about
Reducing their unwanted stout.
None of the people he could see
"Is quite" (he said) "as fat as me!"
Then, with a still more moving
sigh,
"I mean" (he said), "as fat as I!"

Now Teddy, as was only right,
Slept in the ottoman at night,
And with him crowded in as well
More animals than I can tell;

Not only these, but books and things,
Such as a kind relation brings,
Old tales of "Once upon a time,"
And history re-told in rhyme.

One night it happened that he
took
A peep at an old picture-book,
Wherein he came across by chance
The picture of a King of France
(A stoutish man), and, down below,
These words: "King Louis So-and-
So,
Nicknamed 'The Handsome.'"
There he sat,
And (think of it!) the man was fat!

Our bear rejoiced like anything
To read about this famous King,
Nicknamed "The Handsome." There
he sat,
And certainly the man was fat.
Nicknamed "The Handsome." Not
a doubt
The man was definitely stout.
Why then a bear (for all his tub)
Might yet be named "The Hand-
some Cub!"

"Might yet be named." Or did he
mean
That years ago he "might have
been"?

For now he felt a slight misgiving:
"Is Louis So-and-So still living?
Fashions in beauty have a way
Of altering from day to day;
Is 'Handsome Louis' with us yet?
Unfortunately I forget."

Next morning (nose to window-pane)
The doubt occurred to him again.
One question hammered in his head:
"Is he alive or is he dead?"
Thus nose to pane he pondered; but
The lattice-win'ow, loosely shut,
Swung open. With one startled "Oh!"
Our Teddy disappeared below.

There happened to be passing by
A plump man with a twinkling eye,
Who, seeing Teddy in the street,
Raised him politely to his feet,
And murmured kindly in his ear
Soft words of comfort and of cheer:
"Well, well!" "Allow me!" "Not
at all."
"Tut-tut! A very nasty fall."

Our Teddy answered not a word;
It's doubtful if he even heard.
Our bear could only look and look:
The stout man in the picture-book!
That "handsome" King—could this
be he,
This man of adiposity?

"Impossible," he thought; "but
still,
No harm in asking. Yes, I will!"

"Are you," he said, "by any chance
His Majesty the King of France?"
The other answered, "I am that,"
Bowed stiffly and removed his hat;
"But is it Mr. Edward Bear?"
And Teddy, bending very low,
Replied politely, "Even so."

They stood beneath the window
there,
The King and Mr. Edward Bear,
And, handsome, if a trifle fat,
Talked carelessly of this and that...
Then said His Majesty, "Well, well,
I must get on," and rang the bell.
"Your bear, I think," he smiled.
"Good-day!"
And turned and went upon his way.

A bear, however hard he tries,
Grows tubby without exercise.
Our Teddy Bear is short and fat,
Which is not to be wondered at.
But do you think it worries him
To know that he is far from slim?
No, just the other way about—
He's proud of being short and stout.

A. A. M.

Ernest H. Shepard

'Teddy Bear' makes his bow in the pages of *Punch* in February 1924, nine months before the publication of *When We Were Very Young*. The bear who posed for E. H. Shepard in these drawings was not the 'Mr Edward Bear' who lived with Christopher Milne, but 'Growler', a much-loved companion of the artist's son.

Sir Owen Seaman, the editor of *Punch*, had doubts about publishing Milne's 'Very Young' verses, remarking to Shepard: 'You know, these poems are for children, and seem hardly suitable for the pages of *Punch* – however, we shall see.' And see they *did*!

29

'We had sand in the eyes
and the ears and the nose,
And sand in the hair, and
sand-between-the-toes…'

thoughtfully helped him to make a couple of other appearances: lying, with his legs in the air, at the foot of Christopher Robin's bed in 'Vespers', and peering curiously over the top stair in the verse 'Halfway Down'.

The teddy bear in these pictures, however, was not a likeness of the one living in the Milne nursery, whom Ernest Shepard had yet to meet. The artist's model was a bear named Growler, made by the famous bear-makers, Steiff, and belonging to Shepard's son, Graham. 'Growler,' Shepard once said, 'was a magnificent bear. I've never seen his like!' And from the start, the bear destined to become Winnie-the-Pooh had a very particular look about him.

The dedication in *When We Were Very Young* read: 'To Christopher Robin Milne or, as he prefers to call himself, Billy Moon, this book which owes so much to him is now humbly offered.' Methuen were soon asking not for that other detective story, but 'another Billy book'.

Christopher Robin, 'halfway down the stairs', with Teddy Bear (and other unidentified nursery friends) at the top.

30

'Thus, nose to pane,
he pondered…'

As for Teddy Bear, he was beginning to have Ideas of His Own concerning what that book might be about. He also began thinking about the whole business of Names.

Under the Name of Sanders

When Edward Bear said that he would like an exciting name all to himself, Christopher Robin said at once, that he was Winnie-the-Pooh. And he was.

What are we to make of this name, 'Winnie-the-Pooh', which is now so famous that we don't give it so much as a second thought? To answer that, we will have to start at the end of the name, go back to the beginning and then finally sort out the bit in the middle.

A pencil sketch by E. H. Shepard for his illustration to 'The Mirror', A. A. Milne's poem about the swan who was the first owner of the name 'Pooh'.

So, let's begin with 'Pooh', which, rather surprisingly, introduces not a bear, but a *swan* into the story. In 1921, Mr and Mrs Milne and just-one-year-old Christopher had a holiday in the Sussex village of Poling. They stayed in a thatched cottage with a lake nearby; and on that lake was a swan. Christopher, who used to feed the swan, called the bird 'Pooh'.

In his introduction to *When We Were Very Young* (which had included a poem about that swan), A. A. Milne wrote of the name 'Pooh': 'This is a very fine name for a swan, because, if you call him and he doesn't

32

come (which is a thing swans are good at), then you can pretend that you were just saying "Pooh!" to show how little you wanted him.'

Milne went on to explain that, every afternoon, six cows would come down to Pooh's lake, saying 'Moo' as they came. For a versifier it was an irresistible connection: 'I thought to myself one fine day, walking with my friend Christopher Robin, "Moo rhymes with Pooh! Surely there is a bit of poetry to be got out of that?" Well, then, I began to think about the swan on his lake; and at first I thought how lucky it was that his name was Pooh; and then I didn't think about that anymore . . . and the poem came quite differently from what I intended.'

The poem, 'Summer Afternoon', eventually appeared in *When We Were Very Young*, and that is really all that needs to be said on the subject of cows and swans, except that, two years later, when Milne came to introduce *Winnie-the-Pooh*, he started out by referring to that Other Pooh:

'If you happen to have read another book about Christopher Robin, you may remember that he once had a swan (or the swan had Christopher Robin, I don't know which), and that he used to call this swan Pooh. That was a long time ago, and when we said good-bye, we took the name with us, as we didn't think the swan would want it any more.'

And that is how 'Teddy Bear', occasionally called 'Edward Bear' and sometimes known as 'Big Bear' (presumably to distinguish him from the

'Twelve brown cows bend drinking there…
Six from the water and six from the air;'
Shepard's illustration to 'Summer Afternoon'.

smaller members of the species in Christopher's nursery), became 'Pooh'.

So, what about 'Winnie', you ask? In answering that we must begin by quoting Mr Milne once more: 'You can't be in London for long without going to the Zoo. There are some people who begin the Zoo at the beginning, called WAYIN, and walk as quickly as they can past every cage until they get to the one called WAYOUT, but the nicest people go straight to the animal they love the most, and stay there.'

Christopher Robin had often been to the Zoo and Milne had written some verses about those expeditions for *When We Were Very Young*: 'There's a sort of tiny potomus, and a tiny nosserus too – But *I* gave buns to the elephant when *I* went down to the Zoo!' And we've now spent quite enough time with elephants, nosseruses and potomuses, so let's go and see the bears!

'There's a sort of tiny potomus…' Christopher Robin 'At the Zoo' in *When We Were Very Young*.

34

'So when Christopher Robin goes to the Zoo,' wrote Milne, 'he goes to where the Polar Bears are, and he whispers something to the third keeper from the left, and doors are unlocked, and we wander through dark passages and up steep stairs, until at last we come to the special cage, and the cage is opened, and out trots something brown and furry, and with a happy cry of "Oh, Bear!" Christopher Robin rushes into its arms. Now this bear's name is Winnie, which shows what a good name for bears it is, but the funny thing is that we can't remember whether Winnie is called after Pooh, or Pooh after Winnie. We did know once, but we have forgotten . . .'

Milne may have 'forgotten', but history shows that it was definitely Pooh who was called after Winnie. And Winnie, to answer your next question, was a black bear who lived at London Zoo in Regent's Park in an enclosure on the artificial mountain landscape known as Mappin Terrace, 'where the Polar Bears are', or, rather, *were*, in those days when bears were still being kept in zoos.

A. A. Milne told a friend that his son's encounter at London Zoo with the American black bear, Winnie, had inspired him to write a couple of poems – and, possibly, even a story. True or not, *Now We Are Six*, published in 1927, contained 'Furry Bear', a verse in which the poet imagines what it would be like to *be* a bear.

No one seems quite sure when or how often Christopher Robin visited Winnie. According to the late Laurence Irving, one of Milne's friends at London's Garrick Club, the expedition was part of a birthday treat for his young daughter, Pamela, who was accompanied by Anne Hastings Turner, the daughter of another Garrick friend, and 'Billy' Milne.

Years later, Irving wrote to *The Times*, describing how the keeper had conducted the party 'into a dark cavern leading to the grill of Winnie's cage. When he opened it Winnie, as was her custom, ambled out to greet her visitors. No doubt in the narrow confines of the tunnel, to the children she appeared monstrous. The girls held their

ground. Billy wavered, retreated a step or two, then overcame his awe and joined the girls in feeding and making much of the docile bear.' But did Billy *really* 'waver'? Years later, Christopher admitted to having been nervous of those nearby polar bears, but maintained that he had never been afraid of Winnie herself and had revisited this remarkable lady on subsequent trips to the Zoo.

Before ever encountering the docile Winnie at London Zoo, Christopher Robin had heard all about the 'masses of bears' who lie in wait, ready to eat the 'the sillies who tread on the lines of the street', as described in the poem 'Lines and Squares' in *When We Were Very Young*, and which was later included in *The Christopher Robin Verses* (1932) with new, coloured illustrations by E. H. Shepard.

A highly romanticised version of Christopher's meeting with Winnie appeared in an article by the soon-to-be famous children's writer, Enid Blyton, who interviewed A. A. Milne in 1926 and quoted him as saying: 'The bear hugged Christopher, and they had a glorious time together, rolling about and pulling ears and all sort of things.'

As for who actually said 'Oh, Pooh!' you may prefer Mrs Milne's account of it being an ecstatic sigh from Christopher, or Mrs Irving's rather more prosaic version that it was actually said by her daughter, Pamela, in response to the overpowering animal odours in the cage!

Unlikely though it all sounds, and suitably embellished though it

'Just watch me walking in all the squares!' The poem, 'Lines and Squares', as it first appeared in *Punch*, in March 1924, with decorations by Ernest Shepard. The illustration, centre right (showing a bear who has just eaten one of 'the sillies'), would be omitted when the poem was eventually published in *When We Were Very Young*.

Christopher Milne giving 'a little smackerel of something' to Winnie in her cage at London Zoo. And could that be A. A. Milne watching the encounter through the barred window at the back?

Although, as Christopher later recalled, Winnie did not like *honey*, she *did* have a sweet tooth: a photograph in *Secrets of the Zoo*, written by Leslie G. Mainland in 1922, showed a keeper spoon-feeding Winnie (or 'Winifred' as she was called in the book) from a tin of golden syrup. Describing her as 'the tamest bear that ever happened', the book reported that 'children rode on her back and she much preferred condensed milk to raw meat.'

doubtless was, this extraordinary encounter really did take place as can be seen from the photograph, given to me by Mrs Milne, showing Christopher feeding Winnie with 'a little smackerel of something'. Winnie's treat, Christopher later recalled, was not the honey so craved by Pooh, but condensed milk:

> When Rabbit said, 'Honey or condensed milk with your bread?' he was so excited that he said, 'Both,' and then, so as not to seem greedy, he added, 'But don't bother about the bread, please.'

Winnie's story begins in Canada in 1914. Harry Colebourn, a British-born veterinary surgeon, was living in Winnipeg and working for the Department of Agriculture. At the outbreak of the First World War, Colebourn, who was serving with the 34th Regiment of Cavalry (later named the 34th Fort Garry Horse), immediately volunteered to fight for his country.

On 24 August 1914, Lieutenant Colebourn, attached to the Canadian Army Veterinary Corps, set out for Valcartier, Quebec on his way to join the 2nd Canadian Infantry Brigade. The following day, stopping off at White River, Ontario, Colebourn met a hunter who was selling a female bear cub belonging to an American black bear that had just been killed. Paying twenty dollars for the young bear, Colebourn named her 'Winnie' after the town of Winnipeg.

Becoming an unofficial mascot of the 2nd Canadian Infantry Brigade, Winnie accompanied the regiment

Cub cadet: Winnie, the orphaned American black bear cub who would later lend her name to Pooh, during manoeuvres on Salisbury Plain with her friend, Lieutenant Harry Colebourn.

when, in October 1914, it embarked for England. After two months billeted on Salisbury Plain, orders came through for the brigade to set sail for France, and Colebourn gave Winnie – by then a much-loved and pampered pet – into the safe-keeping of London Zoo. At the end of the war, in 1918, Colebourn (now a Captain) returned to England prior to going home to Winnipeg. Although he had originally intended to take Winnie back to Canada with him, the bear had become such a celebrated attraction, that he decided that she should remain in London.

This very remarkable bear lived at the Zoo until her death in 1934, and – in tribute to the helping paw she gave to the creation of Winnie-the-Pooh – a bear cub statue by sculptor Lorne McKean was unveiled by Christopher Milne in 1981, close to Winnie's old home on Mappin Terrace.

So now you know all about 'Pooh' and all about 'Winnie' and only one puzzle remains. It was something which A. A. Milne also wondered about in the opening story of *Winnie-the-Pooh:*

> When I first heard his name, I said, just as you are going to say, 'But I thought he was a boy?'
>
> 'So did I,' said Christopher Robin.
>
> 'Then you can't call him Winnie?'
>
> 'I don't.'
>
> 'But you said—'
>
> 'He's Winnie-ther-Pooh. Don't you know what *"ther"* means?'
>
> 'Ah, yes, now I do,' I said quickly . . .

Part of a 1996 set of Canadian postage stamps commemorating 'Winnie' and 'Pooh'.

'This warm and sunny Spot
  Belongs to Pooh…'
Lorne McKean's bear cub
statue at London Zoo.

41

'Under the name of Sanders…' or, as Shepard has it, 'Mr' Sanders.

And, as if having all those names wasn't enough, we are told, in that first story, that, 'Once upon a time, a very long time ago now, about last Friday, Winnie-the-Pooh lived in a forest all by himself under the name of Sanders.' And in case, like Christopher Robin, you are wondering what 'under the name' means, Milne helpfully explains that it means 'he had the name over the door in gold letters and lived under it.' And, since Pooh never seems to have used the name for himself, that is probably more than enough of an explanation.

Writing of his son, in 1929, Milne explained: 'Like most small boys he has had toy animals to play with, but though he loves them all, his best friend has been his Teddy Bear, called Winnie-the-Pooh, or Pooh, for short. The funny thing is that Pooh doesn't like being called a Teddy Bear now, and if anybody says to Christopher Robin, "Is that your T——y B——?" Christopher Robin says very coldly, "No, it's Pooh," and then Pooh and he go off whispering together. You see, what they both feel and what I feel too, is that Pooh is really alive and does things, but a Teddy Bear is just a toy which sits and does nothing.'

Which means it is now time to find out how it was that Pooh stopped being a toy, came alive and started Doing Things.

After floating up to the top of the bee-tree on the string of a balloon, Pooh's arms were so stiff that 'they stayed up straight in the air for more than a week, and whenever a fly came and settled on his nose he had to blow it off', which prompted A. A. Milne to observe: 'I think – but I am not sure – that *that* is why he was always called Pooh.'

Here We Are ~ All of Us

Christopher Robin was sitting outside his door, putting on his Big Boots. As soon as he saw the Big Boots, Pooh knew that an Adventure was going to happen . . .

'We feel that anybody who could see Pooh, if only for a moment, and not know at once that he was alive, must be a very silly person.' By the time A. A. Milne wrote that, in 1929, there may have been a sense in which Pooh was 'alive', but it hadn't always been the case. True, Christopher Robin's teddy bear may have been a 'special' bear when he arrived in time for the young boy's first birthday, but he was still very much a toy.

The grown-up Christopher Milne would later say of his former childhood companion: 'Clasped in my arms, [Pooh was] not really very different from the countless other bears clasped in the arms of countless other children. From time to time he went to the cleaners, and from time to time ears had to be sewn on again, lost eyes replaced and paws renewed.'

A bear and his boy:
Winnie-the-Pooh posing
with Christopher Robin Milne
in 1928 for photographer
Marcus Adams.

Although chief in Christopher's affections, Pooh shared his young master and the rather cramped accommodation in the nursery ottoman with 'The Others'.

Arriving a few months after Pooh, on Christmas Day 1921, was Eeyore the donkey: grey, certainly, but not yet old and miserable. 'Perhaps in his younger days,' recalled Christopher Milne, 'he had held

44

his head higher, but by the time the stories came to be written his neck had gone like that and this had given him his gloomy disposition.'

More awkward in shape than a teddy bear, the toy donkey was doubtless tugged about by his legs, ears and even his tail: 'They've no imagination. A tail isn't a tail to *them*, it's just a Little Bit Extra at the back.' Such indignities probably accounted for his careworn appearance, just as not being included in as many of Christopher's games as Winnie-the-Pooh no doubt contributed to his sense of being Left Out:

> 'Nobody tells me,' said Eeyore. 'Nobody keeps me informed. I make it seventeen days come Friday since anybody spoke to me.'

Next to come along was Piglet: 'an undated arrival,' wrote A. A. Milne, 'at the hands of a stranger, who had often noticed a little boy walking in the street with his nurse and sometimes stopped and spoke with them.' Piglet's character would emerge as being somewhat excitable and rather nervous ('It is hard to be brave . . . when you're only a Very Small Animal'), but as A. A. Milne would explain in his introduction to *Winnie-the-Pooh*, Piglet enjoyed a special relationship with Christopher Robin:

> Pooh is the favourite, of course, there's no denying it, but Piglet comes in for a good many things which Pooh misses; because you can't take Pooh to school without everybody knowing it, but Piglet is so small that he slips into a pocket, where it is very comforting to feel him when you are not quite sure whether twice seven is twelve or twenty-two.

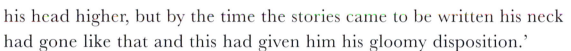

So, there they were: Pooh, Eeyore and Piglet, all three of them, just toys. It required a very particular and collaborative magic to bring them to life.

'It started,' Christopher Milne was to write, 'in the nursery; it started with me. It could really start nowhere else, for the toys lived in the nursery and they were mine and I played with them. And as I played with them and talked to them and gave them voices to answer with, so they began to breathe. But alone I couldn't take them very far. I needed help. So my mother joined me and she and I and the toys played together, and gradually more life, more character flowed into them, until they reached a point at which my father could take over.'

One further ingredient was required: a setting in which these characters might find themselves becoming involved in adventures. In 1925, the Milnes bought Cotchford Farm, in the Sussex village of Hartfield. Thirty-five miles from London, it was the perfect weekend retreat for a town family. There was a garden with lots of potential, which Daphne Milne immediately commandeered as her personal province, with the exception of a rather sad and boggy corner resembling Eeyore's Gloomy Place. There were also lots of winding country lanes leading to tree-crowned hills with breathtaking views where Alan Milne could walk, smoke his pipe and dream up ideas.

'The farmhouse wherein we live is a very old one. None can say exactly how old,' wrote Milne more than twenty-five

Preliminary pencil sketch by E. H. Shepard for one of his illustrations of Christopher Robin and Piglet in *Winnie-the-Pooh*.

years later, 'but because it is still marked as a farm on the ordinance survey map, so it is still known. For ourselves we have bred no more than goldfish.'

For Christopher, after the streets and squares of London, it was a place of great adventure, as he would later recollect: 'There we were with a cottage, a little bit of garden, a lot of jungle, two fields, a river and then all the green, hilly countryside beyond, meadows and woods,

A family snapshot of Christopher Robin (with Pooh tucked under his arm) strolling with his parents in the garden at Cotchford Farm.

47

One of the many sketches made by E. H. Shepard on his visits to the Ashdown Forest.

waiting to be explored; and Nanny and I set out at once to explore them, bringing back reports of our discoveries.'

And as Christopher explored, he began discovering the places that would eventually become landmarks of the World of Pooh. There were the Six Pine Trees, where Pooh and Piglet would dig their Cunning Trap for Heffalumps. There were sandy banks where you found rabbits, or maybe, a very particular Rabbit.

There was a forest, *the* Forest, rising above the valley in which the village of Hartfield and the Milne's farmhouse were cradled. As Christopher Milne later wrote: 'Pooh's Forest and Ashdown Forest are identical.' Here Christopher, the young explorer, might set out on an exciting 'Expotition' – 'Expedition, silly old Bear. It's got an "x" in it.'

On the way he might pass the stream 'which twisted and tumbled between high rocky banks', and the place where Pooh would 'dicsover' the 'NorTH PoLE'.

'Christopher Robin organises an "Expotition".' In 1928, E. H. Shepard painted a series of colour pictures of Pooh and friends to be given away as free prints with the magazine, *Home Chat*.

49

If he climbed long enough, he would come at last to 'an enchanted place on the very top of the Forest called Galleons Lap' (or 'Gill's Lap' as it is marked on the map). Here, in the days before the Terrible Storm of 1987 swept through the Forest, there were 'sixty-something trees in a circle'. It was, as Christopher described it in later life, 'an enchanted spot before ever Pooh came along to add to its magic.'

And as Christopher (accompanied by Pooh) first found that Enchanted Place, so Milne would describe it and Shepard would draw it: 'Christopher Robin knew that it was enchanted because nobody had ever been able to count whether it was sixty-three or sixty-four, not even when he tied a piece of string round each tree after he had counted it . . . Sitting there they could see the whole world spread out until it reached the sky, and whatever there was in all the world over was with them in Galleons Lap.'

On the way down from the Forest, Christopher would have followed the very same forest paths that Pooh would

Sketches by Ernest Shepard of Gill's Lap (above) and (right) Pooh on his way through the Forest to visit Rabbit ('Rum-tum-tiddle-um-tum').

soon be stumping and humming along: 'Through copse and spinney marched Bear; down open slopes of gorse and heather, over rocky beds of streams, up steep banks of sandstone into the heather again; and so at last, tired and hungry, to the Hundred Acre Wood.'

And there, in what was really the *Five* Hundred Acre Wood, was a big tree with a branch that snaked down to the ground, up which an adventurous explorer might climb to the trunk and where, as Christopher was to recall, one might, in imagination at least, find 'a door with a knocker and a bell, a door in the tree and someone living behind it. Who? Who? Could it be an owl?'

Owl lived at The Chestnuts, an old-world residence of great charm, which was grander than anybody else's.

In the stories, Christopher Robin lives (like Pooh, Piglet and Owl) in a house in a tree. While this was just a storyteller's conceit, the real Christopher Robin did have a tree house of his own in the garden at Cotchford Farm. An ancient walnut, hollow inside, it had a great opening in its trunk that was like a door.

Pooh, Kanga and Christopher
Robin photographed in
Pooh's House: the hollow
walnut tree in the garden
at Cotchford Farm.

'It was,' Christopher wrote later, 'the perfect tree house for a five year old. I could climb inside and sit on the soft, crumbly, floor. In the walls there were cracks and ledges where things could be put; and high above my head was a green and blue ceiling of leaves and sky. Pooh and I claimed it. It was Pooh's House, really, but there was plenty of room for us both inside, and here we came to play our small, quiet, happy games together.'

And eventually, those games would become part of the stories to be found in the book that was to be named after its central character – *Winnie-the-Pooh*.

A. A. Milne was to write of the
fictional Christopher Robin:
'To me he was, and remained,
the child of my imagination.
When I thought of him, I
thought of him in the Forest,
living in his tree as no child
really lives…' Which was also
how Ernest Shepard was to
draw him in the Pooh books.

Tell Winnie-the-Pooh a Story

Sometimes Winnie-the-Pooh likes a game of some sort when he comes downstairs, and sometimes he likes to sit quietly in front of the fire and listen to a story.

There was no sign of Pooh. Daphne Milne looked round the nursery but couldn't see the beloved bear anywhere. 'Where's Winnie-the-Pooh?' she asked Christopher Robin. 'Behind the ottoman,' replied his owner coldly. 'Face downwards. He said he didn't like *When We Were Very Young.*' Reporting this story, many years later, A. A. Milne remarked that 'Pooh's jealousy was natural. He could never quite catch up with the verses . . .' However, in 1925, Mr Milne tried to make amends:

'What about a story?' said Christopher Robin.
'*What* about a story?' I said.
'Could you very sweetly tell Winnie-the-Pooh one?'
'I suppose I could,' I said. 'What sort of stories does he like?'
'About himself. Because he's *that* sort of Bear.'
. . . 'I'll try,' I said.

But it really wasn't easy and it nearly came out differently.

The London *Evening News* wanted a new A. A. Milne story for their Christmas Eve edition. So, as he had done many times before, Milne sat at his desk, racking his brains, wondering if an idea would come along. But it wouldn't. Even long Thinking Walks didn't help.

Of course, he had written stories before that were (more or less) for children. There was *Once On A Time*, that almost-fairy-story from all those years before. Yes, that was the sort of thing: Enchantments, Cloaks of Darkness, Magic Swords and Seven-League Boots. Just what the young readers of the *Evening News* would enjoy on Christmas Eve.

He had told plenty of stories like that to Billy Moon and some had even found their way into books and magazines. There was a story about *Prince Rabbit* ('Once upon a time there was a King who had no children . . .') and another one about *The Princess Who could Not Laugh*: 'There was once a King

WINNIE THE POOH
WITH A.A. MILNE AND CHRISTOPHER ROBIN

COPYRIGHT

COSTER

Autographed by A. A. Milne, this postcard reproduces Howard Coster's famous photograph of Winnie-the-Pooh with Christopher Robin and his father. Years later, Christopher Milne would express dislike for this picture that was clearly 'posed' and suggested an intimacy between father and son that was not really true to life.

The storyteller: a drawing of A. A. Milne by E. Heber Thompson, based on one of Howard Coster's photographs.

who had an only daughter, the pride of his heart. She was sweet, she was good, she was beautiful, and the king would have said that she was perfection itself, but for one thing. She never laughed. Nothing seemed to amuse her . . .'

As the December days passed it was Mr Milne who remained un-amused. Daphne told him it was easy. Alan Milne knew otherwise, and then he had a Thought. There *was* a story, but not about Kings and Princesses and all those things you always find in fairy-tales. This was 'a real story', a story about Billy's bear — about Winnie-the-Pooh. So that is the story he started to write: 'This is Big Bear, coming downstairs now, bump-bump-bump, on the back of his head, behind Christopher Robin.'

To begin with he was 'Big Bear' rather than 'Edward Bear', as he was called in the published book, but then it always took time to get names sorted out. When Milne reached the first formal introduction to *Winnie-the-Pooh* he wrote it down as 'Winnie-the-*pooh*' with a small 'p'. As Pooh himself might

'Here is Edward Bear, coming downstairs now, bump, bump, bump, on the back of his head, behind Christopher Robin.'

The opening words of a classic: the first page of the original manuscript of *Winnie-the-Pooh* in A. A. Milne's spidery handwriting.

say: 'It's good spelling but it Wobbles . . .' Anyway, even though A. A. Milne didn't yet know it, he had just written the very first chapter of *Winnie-the-Pooh*.

On 24 December 1925, the tale of Pooh's quest for honey (with the help of a balloon) and his encounter with some suspicious bees, duly appeared with a suitable hoop-la! There was a headline on the front page of the *Evening News*:

And, on page seven, also in Big Letters, the three words:

'WINNIE - THE - POOH'

On Christmas Eve, 1925, A. A. Milne, Christopher Robin and Winnie-the-Pooh were making headlines!

At 7.45pm the following evening, the story of Pooh and the bees reached an even wider audience when it was read 'as part of the Christmas Day wireless programme', by the distinguished actor-manager Donald Calthrop, who Milne had doubtless seen in numerous productions including *Peter Pan* and other plays by J. M. Barrie.

The publication of the story in the *Evening News* was accompanied by an illustration of Christopher Robin holding his pop-gun and the balloon, watching Pooh rolling in the mud in order to complete his disguise as a small black rain cloud. Pooh and his owner didn't look quite themselves on account of the fact that they had been drawn for the occasion, not by E. H. Shepard, but by another noted illustrator of children, J. H. Dowd. Perhaps E. H. Shepard was doing something else and didn't have the time. 'GON OUT BACKSON BISY BACKSON', as Christopher Robin wrote when he was busy in the mornings.

58

However, there was no doubting that E. H. Shepard would eventually illustrate the book, when it *became* a book, as it was obviously now going to do. Just as it had done with the verses, one thing, or one idea, led to another. You start writing: 'Edward Bear, known to his friends as Winnie-the-Pooh, or Pooh for short, was walking through the Forest one day, humming proudly to himself . . .' and it turns into a story 'in which Pooh goes visiting and gets into a tight place'. The sorry tale of a Wedged Bear in Great Tightness was published in a magazine called *Eve* in January 1926. It was now perfectly clear that the new 'Billy Book' which Milne had been promising his publishers was going to be as much about Winnie-the-Pooh as it was about Christopher Robin, and, of course, the Others. With each new episode, Christopher's nursery companions successively made their bow: Piglet in his anxious-making adventure in pursuit of Hostile Animals at that spot in the Forest 'where [as it turned out] the Woozle *wasn't*'; and gloomy old Eeyore losing the tail of which he was fond, indeed, to which he was attached:

J. H. Dowd's illustration of Pooh and Christopher Robin for the *Evening News*, was later used as the cover design for a Pooh story-book, published in America in 1944.

'Somebody must have taken it,' said Eeyore. 'How Like Them,' he added, after a long silence.

There was also a Rabbit and an Owl (Milne called them 'my own unaided work'), respectively bossy and pompous, who, but for their fur and feathers, might easily have been characters in one of the author's earlier plays or stories.

And, specially purchased from Harrod's toy department, there were Kanga and Roo: 'carefully chosen,' said Milne, 'with the idea of not only giving pleasure to the reader, but also fresh inspiration to the chronicler of their adventures.'

Kanga, who originally was to have been a 'he', not a 'she', appeared for the first time, along with Baby Roo, in the seventh story, by which time the escapades of Pooh and his friends were being previewed month by month in another popular periodical of the day, the *Royal Magazine.*

Had Rabbit (aided by Pooh and Piglet) succeeded in his sinister plot to drive the newcomers out of the Forest it would have been a brief appearance indeed, but Kanga was made of sterner stuff and, as so often happens in the stories, all's well that ends well. As a result, Christopher had two new toys to play with and Mr Milne two new characters to write about.

Looking back, more than ten years later, on the the business of writing the stories, Milne said of the toys: 'They were what they are for anyone to see; I described, rather than invented them.' That was how

The toys that inspired the stories: Winnie-the-Pooh, Kanga, Piglet and Eeyore, photographed with Tigger, who would make his appearance in the second book of adventures, *The House at Pooh Corner*. From the collection of the Central Children's Room, Donnell Library Center, The New York Public Library.

Milne put things, modestly, almost as though he hadn't really had much to do with it. He went on: 'My collaborator,' (by which he meant Daphne), 'had already given them individual voices, their owner,' (Christopher, of course), 'by constant affection had given them the twist in their features which denoted character, and Shepard drew them, as one might say, from the living model.'

The author was particularly keen that the toys be 'drawn from life'. At the beginning of March 1926, he wrote to Shepard: 'Hadn't you better come and see me on Thursday sometime?' And, two days later, 'I think you must come on Thursday, if only to get Pooh's and Piglet's likeness, (and I want Piglet quite small – as you will see when you read the sixth story).'

The sixth story was the one in which Eeyore had a birthday and Piglet gave him a balloon which, had he not fallen down on the way and burst it, would have been, as he told the crestfallen Eeyore – 'About as big as me.'

So, Ernest Shepard duly visited, and sketched, Christopher's toys: Piglet, Eeyore and the newly-acquired Kanga and Roo. He also drew Pooh, although he already had a model for *that* character in Graham Shepard's bear, Growler, who had previously posed for the drawings of 'Teddy Bear' in *When We Were Very Young*.

When the Milne family went back down to the country, the artist visited the author at Cotchford Farm where, as he wrote in a letter to me years later, 'I made sketches of the pine trees and the spots that figured in his stories.' Shepard's evocative illustrations capture the beauty of the Sussex countryside and give a dreamy realism to the stories. The toys are toys (except for Rabbit and Owl, of course, and they began to look a little less like forest animals as the stories went on) but they all live in an authentic forest, Ashdown Forest, glimpsed in all kinds of weather.

A. A. Milne was essentially a playwright. He filled the Pooh stories with dialogue and didn't much bother about descriptions of the settings. It was Shepard who added that dimension and brought the toys to life with a sharpness of characterisation that allows them to be both toys and, in a funny sort of way, people as well. We love the characters for the silly things they do and the funny things they say, but we also love them because of the way they look as Shepard drew them. Especially Pooh. Even if he didn't resemble Christopher Robin's bear, he *was* Pooh.

Where it all happened:
Ashdown Forest and one
of E. H. Shepard's sketches
made on the spot where
Pooh's adventures took place.

63

Ernest Shepard drew these rarely-seen pictures of Christopher Robin and Pooh for the poem, 'The Friend', which was first published in the *Royal Magazine* in 1927, and later included (without these illustrations) in *Now We Are Six*.

Christopher himself admitted that, years later, when he wrote: 'What is it that gives Pooh his particularly Poohish look? It is the position of his eye. The eye that starts as quite an elaborate affair level with the top of Pooh's nose and ends up as a dot level with his mouth. And in that dot the whole of Pooh's character can be read.'

Mr Milne and Mr Shepard were not especially close. 'I never knew him intimately,' said Shepard, 'It was difficult to get beyond the façade . . .' And yet, together, they created something unique.

The book of *Winnie-the-Pooh* was published on 14 October 1926 and it was dedicated, in verse, to Daphne:

Hand in hand we come,
        Christopher Robin and I
To lay this book in your lap.
        Say you're surprised?
        Say you like it?
        Say it's just what you wanted?
            Because it's yours –
            Because we love you.

A gift for Mrs Milne it may have been, but Winnie-the-Pooh was also a gift to the world.

Pooh Thought it Was a Different Book

Wherever I am, there's always Pooh,
There's always Pooh and Me.
Whatever I do, he wants to do . . .

While *Winnie-the-Pooh* had been well received ('Almost never has there been so much funniness in a book,' enthused one reviewer); sales initially failed to match those for *When We Were Very Young.* So, in 1927, in response to the demand for another book of verse, Methuen published A. A. Milne's *Now We Are Six.*

Although it was obviously a sequel to *When We Were Very Young,* and might, therefore, have been expected to be mostly about Christopher Robin, there was no keeping Pooh out. Sometimes it was Mr Milne who invited him into the verses, sometimes it was Mr Shepard who worked him into the pictures.

With the publication of *Winnie-the-Pooh*, E. H. Shepard's illustrations had become more than just 'decorations'; they were now part of a co-creation. Quick to acknowledge Shepard's contribution, Milne generously arranged for the artist to receive a share of the author's royalties and, on the publication of *Winnie-the-Pooh*, inscribed a copy with a personal verse, that expressed his admiration for the illustrator he had once dismissed as 'hopeless':

When I am gone,
Let Shepard decorate my tomb,
And put (if there is room)
Two pictures on the stone:
Piglet from page a hundred and eleven,
And Pooh and Piglet walking (157) . . .
And Peter, thinking that they are my own,
Will welcome me to Heaven.

In a 'P.S.' to his Introduction to *Now We Are Six*, Milne wrote: 'Pooh wants us to say that he thought it was a different book; and he hopes you won't mind, but he walked through it one day, looking for his friend

'These are my two drops of rain
Waiting on the window-pane.

I am waiting here to see
Which the winning one will be.'

Piglet, and sat down on some of the pages by mistake.' While there, he posed for Mr Shepard.

Very occasionally, Ernest Shepard draws Pooh as if he were nothing more than a mere stuffed toy, endowed with none of the life demonstrated by Teddy Bear in *When We Were Very Young*. For example, in one of the decorations for the poem 'Busy', Pooh is part of a jumble of toys tied onto a chair, which Christopher Robin (pretending to be an elephant) is carrying on his back. However, a very different Pooh, much more like the Winnie-the-Pooh who normally resides in the 100 Aker Wood, is found in the illustrations to 'Forgotten' consorting with the other 'Lords of the Nursery' (a motley bunch of clowns, kings, rabbits, ducks and a donkey on wheels) and anxiously watching for their young master to return. And it is this Pooh, accompanied by Piglet, Eeyore, Kanga (and, presumably, Roo), who joins Christopher Robin in 'Waiting at the Window' to view the race between James and John, the raindrops.

As with *When We Were Very Young* many of the poems were either about the real Christopher Robin or about the author when *he* was a child. Others, however, were about children in general, any of which (for the purposes of a good rhyme) might be *called* 'Christopher Robin' or be accompanied by an illustration of someone who looked like him.

68

'Lords of the Nursery
Looked down the hill,
Some saw the sheep-fold,
Some saw the mill…'

Ernest Shepard's colour illustration for the poem 'Forgotten', one of twelve plates made in 1932, for *The Christopher Robin Verses*. The view of the hamlet below the hill may have been inspired by the Sussex village of Hartfield where Pooh and the Milne family had their country home, Cotchford Farm.

69

Consider the illustrations to 'The Engineer' ('Let it rain! Who cares? I've a train upstairs'). Pooh and the others, seen queuing for their 'TIKITS' and waiting on the station platform for the toy train, certainly look themselves, but is the young railwayman *really* Christopher Robin?

It seems that Pooh and his fellow travellers will wait in vain since the train, which can only be stopped by the use of a brake made from

Although the illustrations suggest that 'The Engineer' was Christopher Robin, he later denied that he ever owned a toy train, let alone made a brake 'from a string sort of thing'!

'a string sort of thing', has obviously defeated the skills of the engineer: 'It's a good sort of brake but it hasn't worked yet.'

In later life, Christopher Milne who, from childhood, was good with his hands, publicly denied his role in this poem which he felt had libelled his younger self: 'If I'd had a train (and I didn't have a train) any brake that I'd wanted to make for it – any simple thing like a brake – WOULD HAVE WORKED.'

Another poem, unlikely though it may seem, was definitely 'drawn from life'. The illustration to 'Knight-in-armour' shows an astonished Pooh and an apprehensive Piglet watching Christopher Robin, in breast-plate and helmet drawing on a pair of gauntlets prior to mounting a rocking-horse. Pooh and Piglet may look surprised, but Christopher Milne really *did* have his own personal suit of shining armour. A present for his fifth birthday, it had a breast-plate, a back-plate, 'wonderful things that protected my arms,' as Christopher later recalled, '(even though slightly scratchy round the wrist)', and a helmet with a red plume and a visor 'that I could pull down when danger threatened.'

> Whenever I'm a shining Knight,
> I buckle on my armour tight;
> And then I look about for things,
> Like Rushings-out, and Rescuings,
> And Savings from the Dragon's Lair,
> And fighting all the Dragons there.

Whereas the verses in *When We Were Very Young* had mostly been about life-in-the-town, those in *Now We Are Six* featured town *and* country. In 'The Morning Walk' Shepard shows us Christopher and his friend Anne (dutifully chaperoned by Pooh), taking the air in a London park; while in 'Buttercup Days', he depicts the children in one of the fields behind Cotchford Farm.

Anne, who was the daughter of Milne's friend, the theatre critic, W. A. Darlington, was a few months older than Christopher but became (after Pooh) his closest friend. To Alan and Daphne Milne, Anne was almost a surrogate daughter and, as Christopher later put it, the 'Rosemary' that he had turned out *not* to be!

Milne's dedication in *Now We Are Six* reads: 'To Anne Darlington, now she is seven and because she is so speshal'; and Mr and Mrs Milne had hopes that the childhood friendship between Anne and their son would one day flourish and become love. Though it was not to be, this

wish was certainly hinted at in the poem 'Buttercup Days':

> Where is Anne?
> Walking with her man.
> Lost in a dream,
> > Lost among the buttercups.

Pooh and Christopher Robin's life at Cotchford Farm found its way into several of the verses in *Now We Are Six*. Their daring quest for dragons in 'Us Two' is a fanciful reference to a fallen tree which crossed the stream not far from the house and which Christopher had dubbed 'Dragon's Bridge'. 'There could be no doubt about it,' he later wrote, 'there was the great blunt snout raised above the bank, there was the eye, round, hollow, staring; there was the branching wing, ready to beat the air; there was the leg poised above the water; and there was the great, green, scaly back down which you could, if you were very careful, clamber until you were right across to the other side.' And *on* the other side there was a farm full of chickens (or, as Shepard drew them, turkeys), who would get

A. A. Milne photographed outside Cotchford Farm, the family's Sussex home, which also features in E. H. Shepard's illustration (right) to the poem, 'Buttercup Days' in *Now We Are Six*.

very agitated by the two dragon hunters:

> We crossed the river and found a few –
> 'Yes, those are dragons all right,' said Pooh.
> 'As soon as I saw their beaks I knew.
> That's what they are,' said Pooh, said he.
> 'That's what they are,' said Pooh.

One day, Pooh and Christopher, accompanied by Nanny, were explor-ing nearby Posingford Wood, when they came upon an elderly man burning wood to make charcoal. Christopher later recalled: 'While Nanny, good at talking to people, talked to him, I, good at listening, lis-tened.' Later the young boy returned home to tell his father (always looking for a new subject for a poem) all about the charcoal-burner who lived 'alone in the Forest' with 'tales to tell.'

There were also tales to tell about Pooh, and A. A. Milne had already begun to think up ideas for another collection of stories about the Bear of No Brain at All. In the meantime, there was really no

'The charcoal-burner has
tales to tell . . .'

74

keeping him out of *Now We Are Six*. Thanks to E. H. Shepard, he is discovered coming face to face with his famous namesake at London Zoo in the illustrations to a remarkably Poohish 'Hum', entitled 'Furry Bear'.

If I were a bear,
　And a big bear too,
I shouldn't much care
　If it froze or snew;
I shouldn't much mind
　If it snowed or friz –
I'd be all fur-lined
　With a coat like his!

Elsewhere he appeared by name, as the very particular companion of Christopher Robin:

There are lots and lots of people who are always asking things,
Like Dates and Pounds-and-ounces and the names of funny Kings,
And the answer's either Sixpence or A Hundred Inches Long.
And I know they'll think me silly if I get the answer wrong.

So Pooh and I go whispering, and Pooh looks very bright,
And says, 'Well, *I* say sixpence, but I don't suppose I'm right.'
And then it doesn't matter what the answer ought to be,
'Cos if he's right, I'm Right, and if he's wrong, it isn't Me.

Three Cheers for POOH

However, a shadow was already beginning to fall across the sunny world of Christopher Robin. Clouds were gathering: the clouds of education and learning. As Eeyore would put it to Piglet: 'all the things that you and Pooh haven't got.' A time was coming when Christopher Robin would no longer be doing 'Nothing' and when his adventures with 'the Best Bear in All the World' would have to come to an end.

Once Again and For the Last Time

*We will call this Pooh Corner. I could call
this place Poohanpiglet Corner if Pooh Corner
didn't sound better, which it does, being smaller
and more like a corner.*

The American journalist knew that she had scooped a story: 'Pooh has been told,' wrote Mary Lamberton Becker, 'that there will be no more books about him after the one that is just coming. I do not know if he has quite taken it in: ideas come rather slowly to Pooh . . .'

Winnie-the-Pooh, Christopher Robin and his parents were getting rather used to being celebrities. Lots of child-readers (and quite a few grown-up ones) wrote letters to Christopher asking after Pooh, and, sometimes, admirers even sent him presents such as a large toy 'Piglet' who was given the name 'Poglet' and, as Christopher later recalled, 'was much more hand-some, indeed frankly much more appealing and lovable, than my one (who was anyway, by this time, in a rather dog-bitten state).'

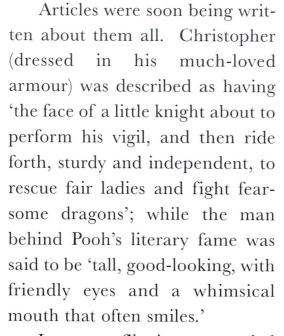

Daphne Milne and Christopher are caught in a family snapshot taken at Cotchford Farm.

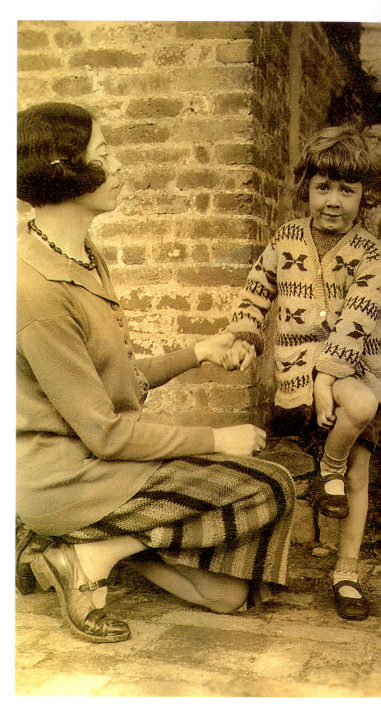

Articles were soon being written about them all. Christopher (dressed in his much-loved armour) was described as having 'the face of a little knight about to perform his vigil, and then ride forth, sturdy and independent, to rescue fair ladies and fight fearsome dragons'; while the man behind Pooh's literary fame was said to be 'tall, good-looking, with friendly eyes and a whimsical mouth that often smiles.'

In one profile, it was revealed that 'Pooh sits by Christopher Robin's bed all night and guards his handkerchief'; in another, it was reported that, for some time, Pooh had lacked one of his eyes ('giving him a rakish and knowing look'), but that it had recently been restored, resulting in a slightly puzzled expression of 'a most moving candour.'

Now, a disappointed world was told that Pooh was about to retire from literary life with a

fourth and final book, called *The House at Pooh Corner*. It was a book of which A. A. Milne would always be proud and which he once described as his 'best work'. He was probably right: it had all the wit and invention of *Winnie-the-Pooh* and more besides. There was also a gloriously stripy (and very bouncy) newcomer to add excitement to the proceedings:

> 'I'm Pooh,' said Pooh.
>
> 'I'm Tigger,' said Tigger.
>
> 'Oh!' said Pooh, for he had never seen an animal like this before. 'Does Christopher Robin know about you?'
>
> 'Of course he does,' said Tigger.

Like Kanga and Roo before him, Tigger had arrived (as Christopher Robin would have put it) 'in the Usual Way, if you know what I mean, Pooh.' And, once again, the 'Usual Way' meant that Alan Milne and his wife, Daphne, had paid another visit to Harrod's toy department.

Tigger first bounced into view in A. A. Milne's story 'Tigger Comes to Breakfast' published in *Sails of Gold*, a children's annual edited by Lady Cynthia Asquith with illustrations by A. H. Watson, who drew Tigger with a far more 'tigerish' look than E. H. Shepard was to give him when the book was published in October 1928.

From the very beginning, it is clear that Tigger is going to be a memorable character:

He was the sort of Tigger who was always in front when you were showing him the way anywhere, and was generally out of sight when at last you came to the place and said proudly 'Here we are!'

The secret of Tigger's appeal is his supreme self-confidence ('Tiggers can do everything'), combined with an unfortunate habit of getting into trouble, as when he attempts to prove that climbing trees is what Tiggers 'do best'; or, again when he bounces the hapless Eeyore into the river. Although Tigger denies responsibility ('I didn't bounce, I coughed'), the fact remains that one moment Eeyore was standing beside the river thinking and, the next moment, was *in* the river, unexpectedly, taking part in a game of 'Poohsticks', a normally harmless pastime originating in the pages of *The House at Pooh Corner*.

For centuries before A. A. Milne gave the game a name, children had dropped sticks into rivers from one side of a bridge and then run across to the other side to see which one came out first. In introducing this entertainment to Winnie-the-Pooh and his friends, Milne was originally going to call it 'Poohbridge' (or 'Poobridge' as he mis-spelt it in the original manuscript): a clever name since, like 'bridge' played with cards, it was also a game.

The bridge in question, which is now known (locally and throughout the world) as 'Poohsticks Bridge', didn't always *have* a name. It was just the little wooden bridge by which the

path leading through Posingford Wood to the Forest crossed the stream below Cotchford Farm. It had been built in 1907, by J. C. Osman, Estate Manager for various properties in Upper Hartfield, with the assistance of his farm labourers.

Then along came Pooh and Christopher Robin who, years later, was to write of the bridge and the game: 'It is difficult to be sure which came first. Did I do something and did my father then write a story around it? Or was it the other way about, and did the story come first? Certainly my father was on the look-out for ideas; but so too was I. He wanted ideas for his stories, I wanted them for games, and each looked to the other for inspiration. But in the end it was all the same:

The men who, in 1907, built the little wooden bridge that would become immortalised in *The House at Pooh Corner*.

81

Poohsticks Bridge' is now a celebrated Sussex tourist attraction.

the stories became a part of our lives; we lived them, thought them, spoke them. And so, possibly before, but certainly after that particular story, we used to stand on Poohsticks Bridge throwing sticks into the water and watching them float away out of sight until they re-emerged on the other side.' And in the story called 'Pooh Invents a New Game and Eeyore Joins In', it is the old donkey who, to everyone's surprise, comes floating out from beneath the bridge. While Pooh wonders whether it was a Joke or an Accident, Rabbit decides that the Bouncing of Eeyore is a cue to attempt the *Un*-bouncing of Tigger. Eventually, however, all the animals (even Rabbit and Eeyore) accept Tigger for what he really is: 'a Friendly Tigger, a Grand Tigger, a Large and Helpful Tigger, a Tigger who bounced, if he bounced at all, in just the beautiful way a Tigger ought to bounce.' In the end Everyone learns to get along with Everyone Else:

> 'Tigger is all right, *really*,' said Piglet lazily.
> 'Of course he is,' said Christopher Robin.
> Everybody is *really*,' said Pooh. 'That's what *I* think,"
> said Pooh. 'But I don't suppose I'm right,' he said.
> 'Of course you are,' said Christopher Robin.

82

Unlike the earlier volumes, *The House at Pooh Corner* had not begun with an 'Introduction', but with a 'Contradiction':

An Introduction is to introduce people, but Christopher Robin and his friends, who have already been introduced to you, are now going to say Good-bye. So this the opposite. When we asked Pooh what the opposite of an Introduction was, he said 'The what of a what?' which didn't help us as much as we had hoped, but luckily Owl kept his head and told us that the Opposite of an Introduction, my dear Pooh, was a Contradiction; and, as he is very good at long words, I am sure that that's what it is.

The looming threat of having to say Good-bye gives the book an unsettled, and unsettling, atmosphere. As Rabbit remarks to Pooh: 'What it all comes to is this . . . *What does Christopher Robin do in the morning nowadays?*'

The note on his door read: 'GON OUT BACKSON BISY BACKSON C. R.', and although Owl vaguely assumed that this meant that Christopher Robin had gone somewhere with Backson and that they were busy together, this was a totally inaccurate interpretation. It was left to Eeyore to reveal the truth: 'What does Christopher Robin do in the mornings? He learns. He becomes

Educated. He instigorates – I *think* that is the word he mentioned, but I may be referring to something else – he instigorates Knowledge.'

Christopher Robin had started going to school and the familiar ordered world of Pooh was about to undergo a change. In January 1929, three months after the publication of *The House at Pooh Corner*, the real Christopher (accompanied by Nanny) set off for his first morning at Gibbs day school for boys.

Before long, as he later put it, he was busy (or 'bisy') learning '*mensa* and *amo*, the dates of George I, the shape of North America . . . ' just as the fictional Christopher Robin was discovering about 'People called Kings and Queens and something called Factors, and a place called Europe, and an island in the middle of the sea where no ships came, and how you make a Suction Pump (if you want to), and when Knights were Knighted, and what comes from Brazil.'

His head full of newly acquired facts, Christopher Robin tells Pooh that, although what he likes doing best in the world is Nothing ('just going along, listening to all the things you can't hear, and not bothering'), he is, from now on, 'not going to do Nothing any more.'

For A. A. Milne, the growing up of Christopher Robin marked the passing of his muse. Later, he was to write of the child's world of the imagination: 'As children we have explored it from end to end, and the map of it lies buried somewhere in our hearts, drawn in symbols whose meaning we have forgotten. A gleam from outside may light it up for us, so that for a moment it becomes clear again, and in that precious moment we can make a copy of it for others. But when the light has gone, to go on making fair copies of that copy – is it worth it?'

'What Christopher Robin does in the mornings.' This colour picture by E. H. Shepard was one of a set of nursery prints offered to readers of the magazine, *Home Chat* in 1928.

Another of Ernest Shepard's delightful watercolour paintings of scenes from the Pooh books, given away with *Home Chat* in 1928. This one was entitled, 'Christopher Robin at the Enchanted Place.'

For Christopher, as he later recalled with honesty: 'Pooh was moving into the shadows. For seven and a half years he had been my constant companion; now our ways were beginning to part . . . I was now living in two worlds. In one we could perhaps still meet for a little longer, but in the other I was on my own.'

In the closing chapter of *The House at Pooh Corner*, the fictional child and the real child fuse into one:

'Pooh,' said Christopher Robin earnestly, 'if I – if I'm not quite—' he stopped and tried again – 'Pooh, *whatever* happens, you *will* understand, won't you?'

'Understand what?'

'Oh, nothing.' He laughed and jumped to his feet. 'Come on!'

'Where?' said Pooh.

'Anywhere,' said Christopher Robin.

During the American journalist's interview with Christopher Robin Milne and his father, Mrs Milne had brought Pooh in to join them and, when the subject of Good-byes had come up, added her own particular comment: 'No more Christopher Robin books!' said Mrs Milne. 'Look, Pooh's crying!' And indeed the brown bear in her arms had his paws over his face. But between them his candid eyes look out confidently. Pooh knows that his place in literature is safe.

If, indeed, Winnie-the-Pooh had shed a tear it would have been uncharacteristic. He was an equable sort of fellow, not given to outbursts of emotion. And, anyway, as Mr Milne had made clear in his 'Contradiction', it wasn't really Good-bye, 'because the Forest will always be there . . . and anybody who is Friendly with Bears can find it.'

Ready for Anything

Last week when Christopher Robin said to me, 'What about that story you were going to tell me about what happened to Pooh when – ' I happened to say very quickly, 'What about nine times a hundred and seven?'

Consider the plots and stories to be found in *Winnie-the-Pooh* and *The House at Pooh Corner* and you will find that all kinds of things 'happen' to Pooh and the other residents of the Hundred Acre Wood. Often small happenings, they are, nevertheless, important in that they bring excitements (and, sometimes, alarms) into their safe and secure world. It is how the characters respond to these happenings that makes them what they are.

Some of these 'happenings', it has to be said, are entirely of their own making: they 'organize' Searches, set out on Hunts, go off on Explores and Expotitions, and devise Cunning Traps using Very Deep Pits. But, without doubt, the most disruptive are those over which they have no control, such as the Weather.

Wind and rain, snow and mist are recurrent

themes in the stories, resulting in all manner of Adventures and providing everyone with a never failing Topic of Conversation.

'I shouldn't be surprised if it hailed a good deal tomorrow,' Eeyore was saying. 'Blizzards and what-not. Being fine today doesn't Mean Anything. It has no sig – what's that word? Well, it has none of that. It's just a small piece of weather.'

'In the country,' Christopher Milne would later write, 'the weather matters. In London you only notice the weather when it is very hot or very cold or very wet. But in the country there is weather every day.' And no one knows the truth of that better than the character who is most often *under* the weather – Eeyore:

'It's snowing still,' said Eeyore gloomily.
'So it is.'
'*And* freezing.'
'Is it?'
'Yes,' said Eeyore. 'However,' he said, brightening up a little, 'we haven't had an earthquake lately.'

Earthquakes aside, the Forest does experience a good deal of, what Owl would call Unfavourable Atmospheric Conditions: cold, misty days (suitable only for trying to lose a bouncy Tigger), and days when it rains and rains and rains. On one such occasion, when (again according to Owl) 'the flood-level had reached an unprecedented height' (or, in other words, 'There's a lot of water about'), Pooh finds himself out on a limb with only ten pots of

honey to keep him company, while Piglet is completely marooned with water almost up to his window: 'It's a little Anxious, to be a Very Small Animal Entirely Surrounded by Water.'

There are also 'Blusterous' days, when gales roar among the tree-tops and, if you happen to be as small as Piglet, you can't help wondering what might happen supposing a tree were to fall down when you were under it ('"Supposing it didn't," said Pooh after careful thought'); and then, before you know it, something 'Oo' occurs and *Owl's* tree falls down, not when you're *under* it, but when you're *in* it!

Then there are snowy days ('not to mention icicles and such-like'), when the best thing for keeping yourself warm is to think up an Outdoor Song which Has To Be Sung In The Snow ('tiddely-pom'). Alternatively you could go tracking paw-marks that might possibly have been made by Animals of Hostile Intent and that *could* be the marks of *Woozles*: 'You never can tell with paw-marks.'

'Being fine today doesn't Mean Anything.'
The weather in the Hundred Acre Wood can be very changeable!

'The wind was against
them now . . .'

Apart from the unspecified menace offered by Woozles and other 'imagined' creatures, such as Heffalumps, Jagulars or even the mysterious Spotted or Herbaceous Backson, there is the very real threat presented by those Outsiders who intrude into the ordered world of the Forest.

First on the scene is a creature that whilst being 'Generally Regarded as One of the Fiercer Animals' is, allegedly, only Fierce during the Winter Months, 'being at other times of an Affectionate Disposition.' This animal, of course, is Kanga:

'Here – we – are,' said Rabbit very slowly and carefully, 'all – of – us, and then, suddenly, we wake up one morning, and what do we find? We find a Strange Animal among us. An animal of whom we had never even heard before! An animal who carries her family about with her in her pocket!'

And scarcely has everyone got used to Kanga (and Baby Roo), when who should come bouncing into the Forest but Tigger: 'a very Bouncy Animal, with a way of saying How-do-you-do, which always left your ears full of sand . . .' Certainly, having Tigger around is not easy, especially for someone like Eeyore: 'I don't mind Tigger being in the Forest, because it's a large Forest, and there's plenty of room to bounce in it. But I don't see why he should come into *my* little corner of it, and bounce there.'

92

These arrivals inspire ill-judged Plans to drive Kanga out of the Forest, by kidnapping Roo, and getting the bounces out of Tigger by losing him on a long explore. Although neither venture turns out to be a particularly Good Idea, everything, fortunately, sorts itself out and ends happily.

Nevertheless, the biggest challenge facing Everyone in the Hundred Acre Wood is still that of Putting Up with All The Others. There is Kanga's insatiable urge to be motherly ('Now, Roo dear, you remember what you promised'); Roo's tendency to get over-excited ('Oo, Tigger – oo, Tigger – oo, Tigger!'); and Tigger's reckless boastfulness: ('They're very good flyers, Tiggers are. Strornry good flyers').

Owl has a habit of using long words such as 'Encyclopaedia' and 'Rhododendron' and his fondness for recounting boring anecdotes ('It was on just such a blusterous day as this that my Uncle Robert, a portrait of whom you see upon the wall on your right . . .'); while Rabbit is extremely domineering: 'It was going to be one of Rabbit's busy days . . . It was just the day for Organising Something, or for Writing a Notice Signed Rabbit, or for Seeing What Everybody Else Thought About It.'

Then there is Eeyore's permanently downcast demeanour ('Nobody minds. Nobody cares. Pathetic, that's what it is'); Piglet's lack of pluck ('Help, help, a Herrible Hoffalump! Hoff, Hoff, a Hellible Horralump!'); and, of course, Pooh's much remarked-upon lack of brain: 'I am a Bear of Very Little Brain, and long words Bother me.'

Brain (and the lack of it) has a lot to do with the various problems which arise and which, invariably, are the result of Mistakes and Misunderstandings. As Pooh himself puts it, on one occasion: 'I have been Foolish and Deluded and I am a Bear of No Brain at All.'

It is Winnie-the-Pooh who attempts to practice a Deception on the Wrong Sort of Bees and who, absentmindedly, eats the pot of honey he is taking Eeyore as a birthday present. And it is Pooh, assisted by Piglet, who builds Eeyore a house at Pooh Corner using a 'heap of sticks' from the other side of the wood that, as it happens, is *already* Eeyore's house.

E. H. Shepard's sketch of Pooh calling at The Chestnuts and noticing Owl's curiously familiar bell-pull.

Not that Pooh is the only one to Get Things Wrong: it is Eeyore who finds Owl a new Wolery, which is really *Piglet's* house; and Owl who wrongly uses Eeyore's tail as a bell-pull. Kanga temporarily 'mistakes' Piglet for Roo, and Christopher Robin decides that he is really a relation of Pooh's called Henry Pootle; and Tigger (so confident about Everything) is not only seriously confused about what Tiggers like best for breakfast, but also about their ability to climb trees: 'They're always climbing trees like that . . . Up and down all day.'

There are, of course, also Accidents: 'They're funny things, Accidents. You never have them till

Eeyore joins in the game of Poohsticks, played here on a bridge quite unlike the little wooden one that was used for the original game. Ernest Shepard painted this colour version of the scene for *The World of Pooh*, published in 1957.

95

you're having them.' Which is why Eeyore, while *not* playing a game of Poohsticks, slips (or is BOUNCED) into the river; why Roo, during the Expotition to the North Pole, experiences Sudden and Temporary Immersion in a stream; and why a Very Bad Accident happens to Pooh, when, during the Search for Small, he falls into a 'Heffalump Trap for Poohs' and lands on top of Piglet.

Such occasions, however, can bring out the Best in People. It is Pooh, for example, who rescues Roo and helps Rabbit in 'hooshing' Eeyore to the riverbank: '*Hooshing* me? You didn't think I was *hooshed*, did you? I dived. Pooh dropped a large stone on me, and so as not to be struck heavily on the chest, I dived and swam to the bank.' And, when Owl's tree is blown down, it is Piglet (being a Very Small Animal) who solves the Problem of Escape by doing a Very Grand Thing in squeezing, sqozing and squzing his way through Owl's letter-box.

This particular event, like many others, is eventually memorialised in verse as a Respectful Pooh Song 'written about You Know What'. It is just one of many Hums of Pooh to be Hummed Hopefully to Others in celebration of finding a Tail, discovering a Pole or simply spending a happy morning seeing Piglet. In other Hums, the Forest's resident poet (Pooh) considers how sweet it is to be a Cloud; wonders what

'Christopher Robin gives Extract of Malt all round', painted in 1928 by E. H. Shepard as one of a series of prints given away to *Home Chat* readers.

might happen if Bees were Bears; why a fly can't bird, but a bird can fly, or ponders similar mysteries:

> Isn't it funny
> How a bear likes honey?
> Buzz! Buzz! Buzz!
> I wonder why he does?

Food is of considerable interest to everyone in the Forest: for Piglet, it is haycorns; for Eeyore, a thistle or two; and for Tigger, Roo's Strengthening Medicine. For Pooh, of course, food is a *very* serious

97

There's always time for a Little Something: lunch with Kanga, followed by a 'Very Nearly Tea' with Rabbit and a 'Proper Tea' with Owl!

matter. Breakfast, for example, might consist of 'a simple meal of marmalade spread lightly over a honeycomb or two' and, since his clock stopped at five minutes to eleven some weeks ago, it is (always) time for a little smackerel of something. And the only thing nicer than having a little something, is having it with someone else:

> 'Let's go and see *everybody*,' said Pooh. 'Because when you've been walking in the wind for miles, and you suddenly go into somebody's house, and he says, "Hallo, Pooh, you're just in time for a little smackerel of something," and you are, then it's what I call a Friendly Day.'

Despite their various ups and downs, Pooh and his friends remain just that – *friends*. 'You're a real friend,' Eeyore tells Pooh, 'Not Like Some'; and Piglet, alone in the flood, can't help wishing that Pooh were with him: 'It's so much more friendly with two.' These friendships are secure and lasting, and are the emotional heart of the books:

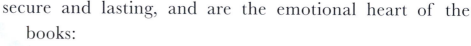

> Piglet sidled up to Pooh from behind.
> 'Pooh!' he whispered.
> 'Yes, Piglet?'
> 'Nothing,' said Piglet, taking Pooh's paw. 'I just wanted to be sure of you.'

At the end of his 'Contradiction' to *The House at Pooh Corner*, A. A. Milne describes Winnie-the-Pooh sitting wakeful on his chair by Christopher Robin's pillow and thinking 'Grand Thoughts to himself about Nothing, until he, too, closes his eyes and nods his head, and follows us on tiptoe into the Forest. There, still, we have magic adventures, more wonderful than any I have told you about; but now, when we wake up in the morning, they are gone before we can catch hold of them.'

The stories, with all their adventures and excitements, may have reached their conclusion, but it was far from being the end of the Things that Happened to Pooh.

Sing Ho! For the Life of a Bear

'It's a Useful Pot,' said Pooh. 'Here it is. And it's got "A Very Happy Birthday with love from Pooh" written on it. That's what all that writing is. And it's for putting things in. There!'

Pooh's Birthday Book, produced in America in 1963, was inspired by *The Christopher Robin Birthday Book*, published thirty-three years earlier in Britain.

The quotation for the twenty-first of August in *The Christopher Robin Birthday Book* reads: 'A very happy birthday, with love from Pooh.' It was an appropriate quotation, since 21 August was the birthday of Christopher Robin Milne. Christopher (or 'Billy' as he was still generally known) was ten years old by the time his father was compiling that book in 1930. Mr Milne was forty-eight and chose as a quotation for his own birthday (18 January) Eeyore's observation: 'Some can and some can't.'

The Christopher Robin Birthday Book ('after all, what *are* birthdays? Here today and gone tomorrow,') was just one of a number of publications that had been developed from the Pooh books within a very few years. Today, a wide range of Pooh novelties are found in bookshops and toy stores, but the Business of Being Pooh began way back in the 1920s. By 1929, Milne's publishers were advertising *The Christopher Robin Calendar* (price 2s. 6d. net), comprising twelve poems with the Shepard decorations: 'Thousands of nurseries will renew acquaintance, day by day, with these old and trusty friends.'

A year earlier, with *The House at Pooh Corner* just published, Ernest Shepard produced six new colour illustrations as nursery prints. These 'Exquisite Colour Plates' (described as 'pictures to love and laugh over') were given free with *Home Chat,* a weekly journal for women. What doting parent could resist the magazine's charming sales pitch: 'Christopher Robin, the delightful hero of the "Pooh" books, has become every woman's little boy, and every woman wants a picture of her little boy to hang upon the walls of her home – a little boy doing those lovable things little boys usually do!' There was also a decorated hanging card of 'Vespers' (price 6d) and

For this nursery print, Ernest Shepard adapted one of his child drawings from *When We Were Very Young* to illustrate the moment when Piglet gets his first glimpse of Christopher Robin's braces and realises just how bracing they are!

When We Were Very Young Notepaper (2s. 6d.), which comprised 'twelve dainty sheets' on which a child could 'send out party invitations and letters under the care of Christopher Robin.'

And, if a party *was* being organised, then tea could be served in a Christopher Robin Nursery Set consisting of cups and saucers, plates, bowls and jugs with hand-coloured pictures of Christopher Robin, Pooh and the other characters, a set of which was presented to the then

The Pooh Party which Christopher Robin gives ('because of what someone did') in the closing chapter of *Winnie-the-Pooh* was to inspire many such events and numerous items of merchandise.

Duke and Duchess of York as a gift for the Princess Elizabeth, later to be Her Majesty Queen Elizabeth II.

In fact, Christopher Robin had been moving in Royal Circles since 1926, when a new and quite different book was published and dedicated to the recently born Princess Elizabeth. Entitled *Teddy Bear and Other Songs from 'When We Were Very Young'*, it contained musical settings for many of the verses.

The composer was Harold Fraser-Simson, who, with his wife, Cicely (and their liver-and-white spaniel, Mr Henry Woggins) lived opposite the Milne family in Chelsea.

Fraser-Simson had achieved a considerable theatrical triumph with the operetta, *The Maid of the Mountains*, featuring the popular song 'Love Will Find a Way', which had opened in 1917 and run for a record 1,352 performances.

When 'Vespers' was published in *Vanity Fair*, Fraser-Simson set it to music for Cicely and when the 'Very Young' verses began appearing in the pages of *Punch*, he pondered setting more of the poems to music. Meanwhile A. A. Milne, who was being approached by a number of composers with requests for the musical rights, began to realise that his 'verses' had the potential to become 'songs', and decided to see whether Fraser-Simson might be interested in the idea.

Fraser-Simson (who as well as being Milne's neighbour was also a fellow member of the Garrick Club) was obliged to confess that he had *already* set one of the verses to music and was thinking about the others! With Cicely singing, Fraser-Simson played Milne his version of 'Vespers' and the collaboration was instantly assured.

Composer Harold Fraser-Simson (known to A. A. Milne and his other friends as 'F-S') and the title-page of his first collection of Christopher Robin and Pooh songs, published in 1924 (left).

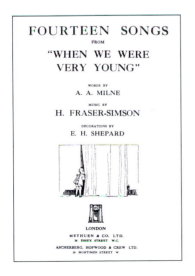

FOURTEEN SONGS
FROM
"WHEN WE WERE
VERY YOUNG"

WORDS BY
A. A. MILNE

MUSIC BY
H. FRASER-SIMSON

DECORATIONS BY
E. H. SHEPARD

LONDON
METHUEN & CO. LTD.
36 ESSEX STREET W.C.
ASCHERBERG, HOPWOOD & CREW LTD.
16 MORTIMER STREET W.

Fourteen Songs from 'When We Were Very Young' appeared in 1924, a month after the publication of the book itself and was followed by *The King's Breakfast* and *Teddy Bear and Other Songs*. Then came *Songs from Now We Are Six*, *More 'Very Young' Songs* and, in 1929, *The Hums of Pooh* with, according to the title page, 'Lyrics by Pooh, Music by H. Fraser-Simson, Introduction and Notes by A. A. Milne,

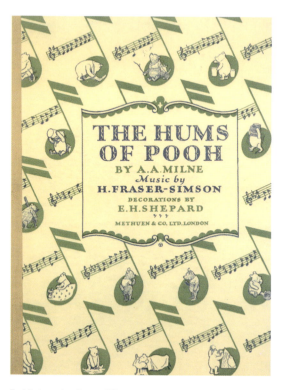

In his introduction to *The Hums of Pooh*, A. A. Milne wrote to Pooh's many admirers: 'Thank you for having loved him. He will be very proud if you sing his songs, and so keep him for ever in your memory.'

Decorations by E. H. Shepard, Additional Lyric by Eeyore.' Fraser-Simson demonstrated in *The Hums of Pooh* an intuitive grasp of Pooh's very particular style of musical composition: 'I shall sing the first line twice, and perhaps if I sing it very quickly, I shall find myself singing the third and fourth lines before I have time to think of them, and that will be a Good Song.'

Milne adopted a tone of mock modesty in introducing the book: 'I was taught in the nursery (perhaps wrongly) that "Self-praise is no recommendation" – (one "c" and two "m's". Some people do it the other way) – but sometimes I think that if one doesn't praise oneself, and there's nobody else noticing, who *is* going to do it?'

He then went on to say that he had come up with a possible solution to this dilemma: 'I did say to Mr Fraser-Simson, "Suppose we have two Introductions, and *I'll* tell everybody how good the music is, and *you* tell everybody how good the words are, and then nobody can possibly say we are being conceited," but he wouldn't. He says he can't write. I suppose he puts two "c's" and one "m" – a pity.'

Milne also added a series of Helpful Notes explaining all about Pooh's Hums and 'just what part of each book each one came in and what Pooh was doing at the time', largely for the benefit of those who had *not* read the books and who might be saying, 'Rumpty Tiddle-y tiddle-y tum, rum tiddle-y tum tum – oh, no it's B *flat* – tum *tum*. A very pretty tune but what's it all *about?*'

'So he sat down on the stone
in the middle of the stream,
and sang another verse of
his song . . .'

Cicely sang each new song as it was written and, accompanied by
Fraser-Simson on the piano, made private gramophone recordings of
the songs, prompting Milne's dedication to *The Hums of Pooh*:

> As Pooh is inspired by a hum or a whistle he
> Hears in the tops of the trees,
> As Eeyore is moved by the crunch of a thistle he
> Pulls at his negligent ease,
> So we were inspired by the humour which Cicely
> Brought to the singing of these.

Christopher Milne, by then seven years old, also found himself being
asked to make a record and was driven to the studios of HMV

'Tra-la-la, tra-la-la,
Tra-la-la, tra-la-la,
Rum-tum-tiddle-um-tum.
Tiddle-iddle, tiddle-iddle,
Tiddle-iddle, tiddle-iddle,
Rum-tum-tum-tiddle-um.'

106

by Fraser-Simson, his nervousness a little eased by having Mr Henry Woggins for company. 'Of course,' Christopher later recalled, 'I didn't have to sing them perfectly. I was a small boy not a professional. A little wobbling on the long notes, a little breathlessness at the end of the line wouldn't matter, might even add to the charm . . .'

The Songs and Hums were soon being professionally recorded by various singers, notably the baritone, Dale Smith, who was followed, over the years, by a diversity of performers from Vera Lynn, 'the forces' sweetheart', to the operatic tenor, Robert Tear.

As for the Pooh stories, they were obviously meant to be read out loud and, indeed, the very first one had been narrated on radio by the actor Donald Calthrop before it was printed in a book. A. A. Milne himself made a recording, reading from the third chapter of *Winnie-the-Pooh* ('In which Pooh and Piglet go hunting and nearly catch a Woozle'), in what Christopher was to describe as 'a dry, monotonous voice' with 'no ups and downs.'

Pooh's exploits clearly lent themselves to dramatisation and the young Christopher Milne found himself involved in a charity matinée performance featuring a version of the episode about Eeyore's birthday. 'Because I was in it,' said Christopher, years later, 'and because I would naturally be taking the part of me, Owl (who appears in the story) had to become Christopher Robin (who doesn't). I still find this a little difficult to explain.'

Any number of stage adaptations were to follow and, eventually (with the help of Walt Disney), a series of animated cartoons. But long before any of

Donald Calthrop (above), gave a radio reading of the very first Pooh story in 1925.

Three Cheers for POOH

Norman Shelley, the BBC's voice of Winnie-the-Pooh also played *another* famous 'Winnie': British Prime Minister and war-time leader, Winston Churchill. Being too busy to make recordings of his famous speeches, Churchill authorised the actor to record them for him!

these, there were wireless dramatisations on the BBC's 'Children's Hour' with veteran radio star, Norman Shelley, in the role of Pooh. A. A. Milne greatly approved of Shelley's performances and, years later, the actor would be called upon to read 'Vespers' and sing 'How Sweet to be a Cloud' at the author's memorial service.

Since Norman Shelley, a host of actors (among them Lionel Jeffries, Bernard Cribbins, Sir John and Hayley Mills, Alan Bennett and Peter Dennis) have read the stories and verses on record and tape.

As for the books themselves, they were available, when first published, in almost as many variant editions as are to be found in today's bookshops. For the very first title, *When We Were Very Young* there were, in addition to the regular trade edition (selling at 7s. 6d.), one hundred copies printed on hand-made paper, signed by the author and artist and costing 42 shillings. With the publication of *Winnie-the-Pooh*, *Now We Are Six* and *The House at Pooh Corner* the collector's market was catered for with both the signed limited, hand-made paper editions and an even more expensive edition of 20 copies (10 guineas each) printed on Japanese vellum!

Whatever editions you might own of 'the Pooh books' (as they were by then generally known), they could be neatly displayed between

Bookends for Sustaining Books ('such as would help and comfort a Wedged Bear in Great Tightness'): a product first marketed in 1930 and still being manufactured, in various new designs, seventy years later.

a pair of Winnie-the-Pooh book-ends (Pooh stuck in Rabbit's front door on one, Owl's 'residence of great charm' on the other): an item of merchandise still being manufactured today, in a variety of Shepard inspired designs.

All kinds of novelties were to follow over the years. There were garden ornaments of Christopher Robin, Pooh and the Others, and, when it was too wet or Blusterous to be out in the garden, there were pop-up books, jigsaw puzzles and board-games, such as 'A. A. Milne's Colorful New Game, *Winnie-the-Pooh*', first produced in America in 1933. According to the game's final rule: 'The Player wins the game whose Playing-

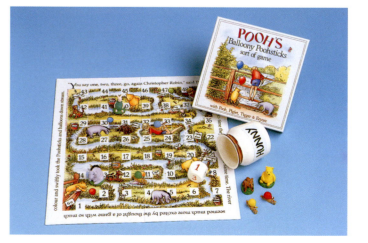

Piece first reaches the North Pole.'

When, in the chapter 'In which Christopher Robin leads an Expotition to the North Pole', the rather surprised Pooh finds that he really has discovered the North Pole, it is Eeyore who asks the awkward question:

'Is that it?' said Eeyore.
'Yes,' said Christopher Robin.
'Is that what we were looking for?'
'Yes,' said Pooh.
'Oh!' said Eeyore. 'Well, anyhow – it didn't rain,' he said.

That is how expeditions (and games) sometimes turn out. That is how Life sometimes turns out. Certainly, that is how it turned out for all the characters, humans and toys, in our story.

The exploits of Pooh and his friends have inspired all kinds of entertainments including board games which were introduced into toy-shops in 1933 and which, with sundry modifications, may still be purchased today.

110

'My tail's getting cold. I don't want to mention it, but I just mention it.'

I'm Not Complaining, But There It Is

So they went off together. But wherever they go, and whatever happens to them on the way, in that enchanted place on the top of the Forest a little boy and his Bear will always be playing.

So, where *did they go* and what *did happen* to them on the way? Well, none of it was quite how anyone might have expected . . . The stories and verses about Christopher Robin and Pooh had been so successful that the little boy and his Bear had become household names. Pooh was so famous in America where the former President, Theodore 'Teddy' Roosevelt, had given *his* name to the 'teddy bear', that children now habitually referred to their teddies as 'Pooh-bears'.

Not all Americans, however, were admirers of the world of Pooh. The poet and wit, Dorothy Parker (who had already denounced Milne's verses in *Now We Are Six* as being 'affected, commonplace, bad,'), attacked *The House at Pooh Corner* in the

'The more it snows, tiddly-pom—'
'Tiddely what?' said Piglet.
'Pom,' said Pooh. 'I put that
in to make it more hummy.'

'Constant Reader' column of *The New Yorker* with a virulent critique on the author's style and, in particular, his use of the expression 'hummy': 'It is that word "hummy", my darlings,' wrote Miss Parker, 'that marks the first place in *The House at Pooh Corner* at which Tonstant Weader fwowed up.'

A highly successful journalist and playwright long before Pooh had come into his life, Milne began to realise that he was now labelled as 'nothing more' than a children's writer. As the years passed, it was a label that he increasingly grew to dislike. Eleven years after the publication of *The House at Pooh Corner*, he would express that dislike in these words: 'It is easier in England to make a reputation than to lose it. I wrote four "Children's books", containing altogether, I suppose, 70,000 words – the number of words in the average-length novel. Having said good-bye to all that in 70,000 words, knowing that as far

Wills's Cigarettes

A. A. Milne

A series of cigarette cards given away in the 1930s celebrated 'Famous British Authors', including A. A. Milne, who was described as having written 'many successful plays and novels', but who was 'particularly well-known for his children's books'.

Despite the considerable burdens which accompanied the fame of being a 'character' in a children's book, Christopher Milne (photographed on the page opposite), became a successful bookseller and, eventually, an author in his own right.

as I was concerned the mode was outmoded, I gave up writing children's books. I wanted to escape from them . . . In vain. England expects the writer, like the cobbler, to stick to his last.'

Writing in his autobiography, aptly titled *It's Too Late Now*, Milne added, with some bitterness: 'As a discerning critic pointed out: the hero of my last play, God help it, was "just Christopher Robin grown up". So that even when I stop writing about children, I still insist on writing about people who were children once. What an obsession with me children have become!' The dramatic work in question was *Michael and Mary*, one of a number of plays, novels and collections of verse and essays that Milne continued to write into the early 1950s. After a long and debilitating illness, A. A. Milne died on 31 January 1956, by which time almost everything that he had written *before* and *after* Pooh had been forgotten.

If the author of *Winnie-the-Pooh* tired of his reputation, so, too, did his son. Although A. A. Milne had once written that he did not want 'C. R. Milne ever to wish that his names were Charles Robert,' that is precisely what happened. Growing up burdened with the name of a child who had once gone 'Hoppity, hoppity, hoppity, hoppity, hop' and who was famous throughout

the world for saying his prayers was anything but easy. Christopher and his parents drifted apart, meeting only once in twenty-five years on Christopher's wedding day in 1948 when he married his first cousin, Lesley de Selincourt. Three years later, Christopher and Lesley moved to Devon and opened a bookshop in Dartmouth.

Many years after, in 1974, Christopher wrote a moving memoir of his life as Christopher Robin. Entitled *The Enchanted Places*, it was dedicated to Olive Brockwell, who before she married had been Olive Rand, Christopher's nanny, herself immortalised in the 'Very Young' verses as the 'Alice' who had taken Christopher Robin to see the Changing of the Guard at Buckingham Palace. The book was full of humour and sadness, some anger and a little bitterness: 'In pessimistic moments,' he wrote, 'it seemed to me, almost, that my father had got to where he was by

'For a long time they looked at the river beneath them, saying nothing, and the river said nothing too...'

In 1979, many years after the invention of the game of Poohsticks, Christopher Milne returned to the little wooden bridge in Hartfield, Sussex.

climbing on my infant shoulders, that he had filched from me my good name and had left me with nothing but the empty fame of being his son.'

Eventually, perhaps through writing *The Enchanted Places*, Christopher found a sense of peace. In his second volume of autobiography, *The Path Through the Trees*, he wrote of his earlier book: 'The writing and its reception combined to lift me from under the shadow of my father and of Christopher Robin, and to my surprise and pleasure, I found myself standing beside them in the sunshine able to look them both in the eye.' In later years, Christopher took part in various Pooh celebrations: cutting the ribbon at the opening of the newly-restored Poohsticks Bridge, unveiling a memorial in a clearing in the Ashdown Forest and the bear-cub statue that was London Zoo's tribute to the real 'Winnie' and the fictional 'Pooh'. Christopher continued to write, living in Devon with his wife, Lesley, and their daughter, Clare, until his death at the age of seventy-five on 20 April 1996.

And what of A. A. Milne's other 'Collaborators'? Daphne Milne, who survived her husband by fifteen years, eventually sold Cotchford Farm in 1964, whereupon that little corner of Sussex, once the home of Pooh, passed into other hands. In the garden there still stood the sundial, decorated with carvings of Pooh and his friends, beneath which, it is said, Milne had buried a first edition of *Winnie-the-Pooh*.

Harold Fraser-Simson collaborated only once more with Milne in composing the music for *Toad of Toad Hall*, the playwright's dramatisation of Kenneth Grahame's *The Wind in the Willows*, that was first staged in 1929.

The name of E. H. Shepard also became linked with *The Wind in the Willows* when, in 1931 he illustrated Grahame's book, and provided definitive likenesses of Mole, Rat, Toad and Badger which, along with those of Pooh and company, are among the most beloved book illustrations of the twentieth century.

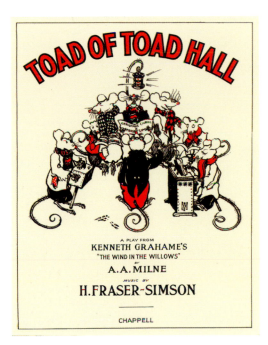

Although Shepard illustrated more than fifty other books, he remained universally known as 'The Man who drew Pooh'. In 1969, he bequeathed 300 of his original pencil sketches to the Victoria and Albert Museum in London, and produced full-colour versions of his line illustrations to both *Winnie-the-Pooh* and *The House at Pooh Corner*. Reflecting on his association with that 'silly old bear', he wrote: 'It was a happy task for me making these drawings and I have grown to love the little folk of these stories.' He was awarded the Order of the British Empire in 1972. Four years later, on 24 March 1976, Ernest Howard Shepard died at the age of 96. Celebrations were just getting under way to mark Winnie-the-Pooh's fiftieth birthday. Shepard's illustrations of Pooh remain beloved by readers and originals are much sought after by collectors: in 2000, a portrait of Pooh in oils,

The cover of Harold Fraser-Simson's musical score for *Toad of Toad Hall*, A. A. Milne's play based on Kenneth Grahame's *The Wind in the Willows*.

This caricatured tribute to E. H. Shepard (and Pooh) was drawn by fellow *Punch* cartoonist, Norman Mansbridge, for the menu of a dinner given by the humorous magazine in 1960.

Pooh portraits: the only known oil painting of Winnie-the-Pooh by E. H. Shepard made for an English tea-shop called 'Pooh Corner', and two of the 300 original Pooh pencil sketches which the artist presented to the Victoria and Albert Museum in 1969.

The original 'Winnie': a statue (opposite) sculpted by Bill Epp and showing the famous bear cub with her friend, Lieutenant Harry Colebourn, was presented to London Zoo in 1999 by the Fort Garry Horse, Colebourn's regiment in Winnipeg, Canada.

which Shepard had painted for a tea-shop called 'Pooh Corner', was sold at auction for the sum of £110,000.

And what of Pooh himself, or the *various* Poohs that we have encountered in the book? Winnie, the American bear cub who loaned Pooh her name, is now commemorated (alongside her friend Lieutenant Harry Colebourn) with statues erected in the Winnipeg Zoo, after which the city she was named, and London Zoo, where she spent most of her life and first met Christopher Robin.

Ernest Shepard, aged 90, working on his colour illustrations for *The House at Pooh Corner.*

As to Growler (the pictorial model for Pooh, who had belonged to Shepard's son, Graham) his fate was not a happy one. 'He was passed on to my grand-daughter, Minette,' Shepard told me, 'a little worse for wear, but still the Best Bear in the World. Minette took him to Canada during the war, and poor Growler came to an untimely end, worried to bits by a Scottie dog in a Montreal garden.'

The literary inspiration, the Pooh who had been boon companion to the young Christopher Robin, fared rather better. When Pooh's owner moved away, he and the Others were placed in a glass case in the nursery at Cotchford Farm. In 1929, Milne had written of the toys: 'I have not created them. [Christopher Robin] and his mother gave them life, and I have just "put them into a book". You can see them now in the nursery, as Ernest Shepard saw them before he drew them. Between us, it may be, that we have given them shape, but you

have only to look at them to see, as I saw at once, that Pooh is a Bear of Very Little Brain, Tigger Bouncy, Eeyore Melancholy and so on.'

And that is how, one day in 1947, they were seen by Elliott Macrae, President of E. P. Dutton, Milne's American publishers. Macrae asked if he might borrow the toys for an American tour and off they all went (well, as we shall see, *nearly* all of them), welcomed to New York at a tea-party organised by the famous store of R. H. Macey & Company and were soon travelling around the States, insured for $50,000 and accompanied by a 'Birth Certificate' from the author

who told the history of Pooh, Eeyore, Piglet, Kanga and Tigger and explained why Roo was missing from the expedition: 'A subsequent dog, who became part of the establishment, took him for a walk once and left him in a hollow tree, from which he was extracted a year later. But the spirit of adventure was now strong upon him, and soon afterwards he was off again – whether or not with the co-operation of the dog this time is not known. The latter was one of those friendly but unbalanced young things who must have company: and if Piglet's face now gives the impression of having seen better days, they were the days before the dog joined the party. But no explanation is needed for the world-weariness of Pooh and Eeyore. Time's hand has been upon them since 1921. That was a long time ago.'

After a decade of personal appearances, the toys ceased their wanderings and, acquiring American citizenship, took up residence in the New York offices of E. P. Dutton.

Pooh (accompanied by his friends) visited England in 1969 for an exhibition of Shepard's drawings at London's Victoria and Albert Museum and on a later, somewhat rainy, outing to the Ashdown Forest (suitably protected by a plastic bag) Pooh helped plant a tree on Galleon's Lap and listened very politely while the author of this book read him the last chapter of *The House at Pooh Corner*.

In 1969, by then the grand old bear of literature, Pooh re-visited his old stomping ground in and around the Ashdown Forest.

Together with his friends Piglet, Eeyore, Kanga and Tigger, Pooh now lives quietly in the Children's Department of the New York Public Library.

In contrast, Pooh the *character* has lead a life filled with activity, busying himself making films and records, appearing in plays on stage,

Pooh also made a personal appearance at London's Victoria and Albert Museum, accompanied here by Kanga and Piglet, for an exhibition of Ernest Shepard's original sketches.

121

television and radio, not to mention inspiring a plethora of toys and games. Pooh is an enduring icon and a merchandising miracle! His likeness is to be found on nursery furniture, children's clothing and just about everything from Special Pencil Cases (with pencils marked 'B' for Bear) to birthday cakes (with or without candles and pink sugar)!

And, of course, books, books, books. Books translated into a host of languages; big books and very small books; books that pop-up; books to cut-out and books to colour-in; books which look, more or less, the way Mr Milne wrote them and Mr Shepard drew them, and others which look decidedly different.

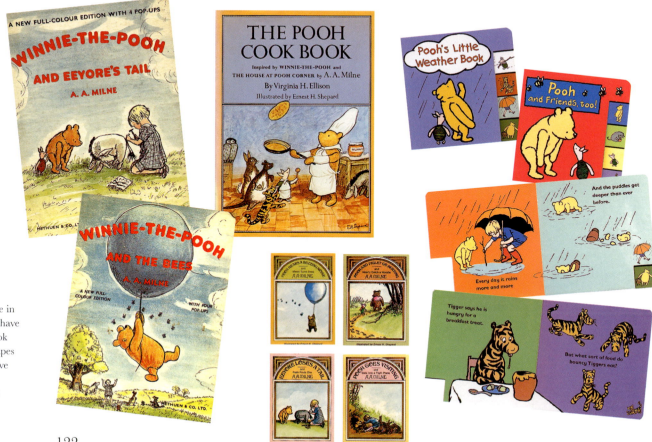

Since his first appearance in print, Pooh's adventures have inspired hundreds of book titles, produced in all shapes and sizes; and, seventy-five years on, his career in publishing shows no sign of diminishing.

Pooh's exploits have inspired theses, manuals and papers by all manner of experts, philosophers, theologians and theorists. And, appropriately for a work by a *Punch* humorist, incidents from the Pooh books have been reworked in words and pictures by several generations of satirists and cartoonists. However, all that, and much else besides, is part of Another Story altogether.

It is enough that, having reached the august age of eighty, without looking a day older or showing any signs of losing his charm or his appeal, we can confidently give him three hearty cheers and hope he'll be with us for years and years:

> 3 Cheers for Pooh!
> *(For who?)*
> For Pooh –
> 3 Cheers for Bear!
> *(For where?)*
> For Bear –
> 3 Cheers for the wonderful Winnie-the-Pooh!

P.P.S. (Personal Post-Script)

'This writing business. Pencils and what-not.
Over-rated, if you ask me. Silly stuff. Nothing in it.'

When *I* was very young, Mrs Bertoletti, a neighbour whose children had grown up and left home, lent my parents copies of A. A. Milne's Winnie-the-Pooh and Christopher Robin books. They were read and re-read so many times that most of the verses (especially the one about 'Bad Sir Brian', *my name!*) and many of the Sayings of Pooh passed into daily family conversation. Then we moved home and the beloved books had to be returned.

Some years later, by which time I was at school (and struggling, like the King of Peru, with 'nine nines are eighty-one, multiply by three'), I re-discovered the Pooh books, which for the first time, were being published in paperback. Delighted at meeting up with the inhabitants of the 100 Aker Wood once more, I enthusiastically embarked on turning *Winnie-the-Pooh* into an end-of-term play. As if my shameful disregard for the laws of copyright wasn't bad enough, I decided that Pooh & Co should be dramatically represented, not as toys, but as eccentric human beings. Casting myself in the roles of A. A. Milne and

Eeyore I called it (somewhat pretentiously) *The Lost Childhood*.

When I was rather older, Miss Baker, another kindly neighbour, gave me copies of *Not That It Matters* and *If I May* in which, for the first time, I encountered Milne, the writer for adults, and fell under the spell of his subtle, ironic wit.

Several more years passed, and, as the Bear of Very Little Brain approached his half-century, I was commissioned by the BBC to write a radio programme in celebration of his birthday. I was given the job on the recommendation of a dear friend, the late Peter Bull (actor and internationally renowned teddy bear authority), who was to be the programme's narrator. Directed by the distin-  guished drama producer John Tydeman, it featured the talents of singer and pianist, Antony Miall, and radio's 'Voice of Pooh', Norman Shelley. It was called (what else?) *Three Cheers for Pooh!*

It was around this time that I began corresponding with Ernest Shepard and with Christopher Milne and his mother. As a result, I started thinking about this book. It seemed a Good Idea and I even talked with Pooh's publishers about it who, like Owl, looked Wise and Thoughtful and said 'I see what you mean. Undoubtedly.' While Everybody was Thinking, I got on with organising a couple of Pooh exhibi-  tions, editing *The Pooh Sketchbook* and *The Pooh Book of Quotations* and privately printing a bibliography of Milne's writings for children.

All the while, however, *this* book was sitting there, waiting to get itself written. And now it *has!* Which means it is time to acknowledge all those people, without whose help and encouragement over the years, it might still be waiting: Joy Backhouse, Pauline Baynes, Anne Clarke, Joan Crammond, Bill Craven, Diane and Peter Dennis, Elliot Graham, Shirley Harrison, Antony Miall, Sue Langabeer, Marilyn Malin, Ann Thwaite, Michael Turner, Mike Ridley, John Tydeman, Joyce Irene Whalley, Joan Wood and Norman Wright; David Boulton, Ian Carter, Brian Denton, Andrew Higgs and Robert Hendry (fellow cast-members of *The Lost Childhood*); Gordon Crossley of the Fort Garry Horse Museum and Archives, Philip Errington of Sotheby's, Michael Brown and Peter Janson-Smith, Trustees of the Pooh Properties, and Elizabeth Stevens of Curtis Brown; the staff of the British Film Institute, London Zoo and the Theatre Museum. Particular thanks are due to Susan Hitches and Ness Wood at Egmont Children's Books, for their painstaking and loving care over the editing and designing of this book; and to my agent Vivien Green, and my partner David Weeks, for all their support and encouragement.

Although I am no longer able to express my indebtedness to them in person, grateful appreciation is owed to the late Olive Brockwell (née Rand), Denis Crutch, Roger Lancelyn Green, Iva Hill (née Osman), Mary Knox (née Shepard), Christopher Milne, Daphne Milne, Norman Shelley, Ernest Shepard and my mother and father.

To all of them (along with Mrs Bertoletti, Miss Baker and Mr Bull) Both of Us – that is Pooh and I – say: 'Thank You for Helping Us Get Here.'

'If anyone wants to clap,' said Eeyore, 'now is the time to do it.'

Acknowledgements

The author and publisher have taken all possible care to trace the copyright holders of all the pictures used in this book, and to make acknowledgement of their use. The list below is as complete as we have been able to make it. If we have omitted to identify any item, we would welcome any supplementary information, which will be used in subsequent editions.

For kind permission to reproduce pictures and photographs acknowledgement and thanks are due to the following:

Rosalind Adams for the photographs by Marcus Adams on pp 9, 22, 23, and 44; The BBC for the photograph of Norman Shelley on p 108; Carlton International for the photograph of Donald Calthrop on p 107; Kyuryudo-Art Publishing Co Ltd., Tokyo for the photographs by Yuji Nakagawa from 'To the Enchanted Places with Winnie-the-Pooh' on pp 10 and 63; Michael Dyer Associates Ltd for the photographs on pp 20, 109 and 110; London Zoo for the photograph of the bear cub statue by Lorne McKean on p 41; The National Portrait Gallery for the portrait by Howard Coster on p 19, and the photograph by Howard Coster on p 55; The collection of the Central Children's Room, Donnell Library Center, The New York Public Library for the photograph of the original toys on p 61; The Walt Disney Company Limited for the postage stamps from the Canadian Post Office on p 40; Pooh's Party Book book ends, produced by Charpente, a division of Michael and Co., on p 109; and for Pooh's Balloony Poohsticks Sort of Game, produced by The Traditional Games Co. Ltd., on p110.

For making the following material available the publisher would like to acknowledge and thank the family of Lt. Harry Colebourn for the photograph on p 39; Dutton Children's Books for the illustrations and photographs on pp 25, 36, 95, 100 and 122; Brian Sibley for the photographs on pp 38, 47, 52, 72, 78, and 116; and Trinity College Library, Cambridge for the photograph on p 57.